"Beautiful! I have read many bo
that had me inspired and crying
done! I give it a Z +!"

**TOM ZIGLAR,**
Proud son of Zig Ziglar

"After reading the book, I was both impressed and informed. Reading
your history, I now understand your motivation! The Fig Factor and
your family have helped you grow to be the successful businesswoman
that you are today. Your book reminds us that the right angle for
approaching a difficult problem is the try-angle."

**- CLARK WEBER,**
WLS Radio celebrity and author of Clark Weber's
Rock and Roll Radio: The Fun Years, 1955–1975

"With rich anecdotes and an honest heart, Jackie's story demonstrates
emphatically that we don't have to be defeated or defined by failure,
disappointment, or hardship. Her life is a testament to resiliency and
optimism. This book should help you realize that, like her, we can all
find the inspired strength within to lead lives dedicated to making
a positive difference. It is more evidence that Jackie Camacho-Ruiz
continues to bless the world, especially those of us privileged to know
her and to have worked with her."

**- BILL MOLLER**
Talk show host, WGN Radio, Chicago

"Sometimes in a barren desert, a flower still grows. Jackie's The Fig Factor is that flower, and how sweet it is! She is not only a dynamic storyteller, but also a person we should all emulate. If you need or appreciate inspiration, I highly recommend that you read The Fig Factor."

**STEVE FRETZIN,**
Entrepreneur and author of Sales Free Selling

"Jackie's heart-wrenching story of a little girl's triumphs in the face of tragedy is a lesson on how your attitude can shape your world. Jackie beautifully paints the picture of how she sculpted her life with the tools of passion, discipline, and gratitude. This gripping book inspires you to look for the good in yourself and others--and strive to make a difference."

**SHEBANI KULKARNI,**
Popular host, speaker, founder of EQuest Global Group and co-founder of The Meadows Club.

# the fig factor

## A memoir about growth, inspiration, and second chances.

by *Jacqueline Camacho-Ruiz*

# *The Fig Factor*

www.thefigfactor.com
www.roundtablecompanies.com

Cover design and layout by Juan Pablo Ruiz,
JJR Marketing, Inc.

Printed and bound in the U.S.A.

ISBN#: 978-1-939418-22-7

Library of Congress Control number: 2013936674

# Contents:

*To Juan Pablo Ruiz, the love of my life, and our two beautiful children, Leonardo and Giulianna, for inspiring me to keep going, and to my mother, Felicitas, for her unconditional love and support.*

# *Acknowledgements*

I want to thank my writer, Michele Kelly, for bringing this book to life with not only her amazing talent but also her ongoing, relentless support and dedication to this project—indeed, the biggest project of my life. Katie Gutierrez of Round Table Companies, Inc. was instrumental as our editor throughout this process, working to ensure that you connect with the story every step of the way. Thanks, Katie, for helping Michele and me on this project from a different, beautiful perspective. We could not have done it without you.

Thanks to my husband, Juan Pablo, for his ongoing support and love and for making me a better person every day. To my children, Leonardo and Giulianna, for being part of our lives and bringing me so much joy.

I want to thank my mother, Felicitas, for exposing me to amazing literature and positivity early on—without her, I would not be where I am today.

I thank my father, Jesus Camacho, for his constant advice on business and life.

Thanks to my two brothers, Efrain and Salvador, for supporting me throughout my life—I could not have been blessed with better siblings.

I am incredibly grateful to all the teachers who believed in me throughout my education. Irene Anzola's beautiful drive to help others inspires me every day. Mrs. Martin kept up with my quest to learn English by patiently feeding me the meaning of every word that intrigued me. I thank them both from the bottom of my heart.

To all my mentors, including Clark Weber, Brian Marshall, Jim Kendall, Marlene Baczek, Joe Abraham, Mario Ponce, Harriet Parker, Sara Victory, Michelle Arden, and Kevin Doyle, among others—thank you for helping me grow.

To my clients, partners, colleagues, vendors, and media contacts—thank you for your ongoing commitment to excellence and success.

And to the countless people in my life who left a lasting impression in my heart—this book is because of you and for you. Thank you.

# *Foreword*

In my experience of working with hundreds of leaders, mostly in the hospitality industry, I have learned that one factor sets great leaders apart from merely good ones: intuition. Their decision making is virtually innate—like a sixth sense. Those of us who study leadership know that much of that intuition is actually by design, built by the experiences that shape each of us. Jackie Camacho-Ruiz serves as an example of how your past shapes your future. This is one reason she has developed into the leader she is today.

What is unique about Jackie is that she is as genuinely optimistic, hardworking, and tenacious today as she was the moment I met her. At the tender, yet highly enthusiastic, age of 21, she yearned for excellence, yet was never defeated by failures. Today, her value system and passions remain intact, her love of family and people is solid, and her commitment to making a difference is unwavering. I often wondered how this young person came to be so motivated. It wasn't until I read this memoir that it became vividly clear: Jackie doesn't take life for granted.

While others might be more interested in hugging the couch, going out every weekend, or just living a "chilled" life, Jackie enjoys life by learning how to make a difference. What makes her story compelling are the rewards she enjoys as a result of the effort. Her willingness to understand the leadership quotient is fascinating and compelling. Strap on your seatbelt—you're going on a journey you won't soon forget.

— Mario Ponce

*Mario Ponce is the principal at Partners in Hospitality, a hospitality consulting firm in Chicago, Illinois. He is the author of the bestselling book Waiting on America and has addressed thousands of hospitality and business professionals.*

# First, A Note

Whenever I speak publicly, my heart takes off like a thoroughbred driven by his rider's urging. People say that even the most famous performers in the world feel this way before they step on stage—kept on their toes by adrenaline. Then, truth meets time. The moment comes when I walk up to the podium, swallow hard, and lose myself in a story so close to my skin that I lose a layer with each experience I share: my mother's painful loss mitigated by my miracle birth; the fire that ravaged my home and left me with love, courage, and hope; the repeated failures in business that grew vast reservoirs of determination; and the figs, those luscious, burnt-colored figs that taught me to pursue greatness amidst odds that were not in my favor.

As a professional speaker and the founder of a major Midwest marketing agency, I give perhaps 150 or so speeches a year, many on college campuses. On April 11, the College of DuPage in Chicago's west suburbs hosted two hundred young people from area high schools to preview the junior college's campus and curriculum. My keynote kicked off their day, with students receiving a copy of my first book, *The Little Book of Business Secrets That Work!* Enamored at being in a collegiate setting, the students were a sea of blue jeans and smiles, flushed with excitement and a real desire to learn. I shared my life experiences, laced with both pain and accomplishment. I was honest when I told them how the challenges of growing up in Mexico gave me the gift of resilience. I did not hold back when I shared my early experiences in an American high school; some of them, I knew, would understand the angst of being ostracized. I opened up my heart because I wanted them to be hopeful and to embrace their future and, even more importantly, their difficulties. I knew how important this was for them. I wanted them to know that life is about second chances, again and again, and that they are, indeed, powerful agents of change.

Then the scene took a right turn. April 11 is my birthday, and as I stepped down from the stage, all those teenagers gathered around me and sang in my honor. My heart swelled, my cheeks flushed, and a rush of gratitude swept across my heart.

In that moment, I realized that my story didn't belong to me anymore; it was bigger than I was. Surrounded by these faces filled with the hope of finding their true purpose, I decided right then that I would offer up my life's journey in a book. I needed to be there for Debbie, Jack, Patrick, Peter, and Austin. Katherine needed to know that she had so much more going for her than she realized. As for Abigail, her fear of commitment didn't have to stop her from letting people help her grow. And Maria? If she just changed her lens from resentment to gratitude, she would find the joy she so desperately sought. The hundreds of young people I met that day inspired me. The longing in their hearts resonated through their hugs, their off-key voices, their smiles, and their stories. I wanted to scream, "I have been there! Everything will be okay and the best of life is all around you right now, right here." We sliced up the birthday cake. I had never tasted anything so sweet.

For me, that day was an awakening, one of many such moments chronicled in these pages. Strung together, they have taught me a valuable lesson: from the depths of struggle comes a wellspring of gratitude that inspires us to be better, happier, more accomplished people.

The day's final imprint on my heart was a self-promise: I would share what I had discovered. I needed to tell people about the figs.

\* \* \*

Long considered a symbol for peace, prosperity, and abundance, figs changed my life. I was not much more than five years old when I noticed these little fruits hanging near the top of a tree outside my bedroom window. Having a flourishing tree to stare at was an anomaly in a city built on swampland and burdened by pollution, yet, somehow, there hung those figs. They whispered to me.

I went to the backyard and regarded the tree with the seriousness of a business partner. The figs swayed a bit in the wind, beckoning me to do something with them, so I climbed the tree, my tiny fists grabbing the fruits and stuffing them in the pockets of my skirt. I brought out a small table and decided to sell them. But nobody stopped to buy them.

Not fair, I thought. The people walking by needed figs. *My* figs. So I brought the figs to the people, chasing passersby and offering five figs for three pesos. I netted thirty pesos that day—a fortune for a child. My return, however, was far greater than the coins in my hand. Those figs had been right in front of me long before I recognized them as an opportunity. How much more could I have done with them if I had seen them—really seen them—sooner? That question launched a lifelong pursuit of living what I call the "fig factors."

My greatest hope is that after you read *The Fig Factor*, a spark will catch. Just imagine if this light illuminated every facet of your life: your relationships, your openness to learning, your acceptance and appreciation of matters great and small, your work, and your creative approaches to challenges. My hope is that your life will never be the same once you regard the world with the wonder and gratitude of a child selling a miraculous little fruit.

Thank you for being here to experience this journey, for sharing in this story that is no longer just my own. Now, come walk with me . . .

# PART ONE:
## *Seeds, the Beginning of Life*

# 1

# BEFORE ARRIVAL

*"On the other side of fear
lies everything you ever wanted."*

— Clark Weber

Mexico City is one of the largest cities in the world—twenty million people scramble to survive, and my family was no different. I remember one funny line people used to say: "To survive in Mexico City, you have to scratch harder than a chicken, move faster than a cat, and sing louder than a rooster." The last one is probably the most important. In Mexico City, if you are not heard, you are trampled on—by people, dust, thievery, and hopelessness.

As unique as Mexico City is, however, some things are universal: people fall in love and people die. People sleep, shop, and worry about their futures. Children play, doctors mend, and mothers pray. And, in mansions or shanties, grief winds its hands around broken hearts and dismantles them carefully.

My mother, Felicitas Esparza, was one who prayed for life. Her quest brought her two sons, followed by two babies lost at birth. Grief found her through physical pain, bloodstained sheets, and the dark dance of physician and nurses tending to death instead of life. The loss of a child disarms us; undeniably, we are changed forever. And so it was with my mother.

With long, shiny brown hair framing her smooth cinnamon skin, my mother's physical beauty was unquestionable. Her true beauty, though, could be found in her deep brown eyes, which swathed her sons in unconditional love. After the loss, her gratitude for the two strong boys she raised was even more pronounced—she was even thankful for the little girl who had not yet entered the world. Her heart beckoned that daughter, and my mother never questioned if —but rather, when—she would cradle that baby in her arms.

Have you ever seen the game where dice are placed under three identical cups? One player switches them around so another player can try to guess which die is under which cup. That's how it was for my mother. Her sadness was always under the first cup. Her stubbornness lay under the second. And, luckily for me, her unmitigated resolve sat solidly under the third cup.

She visited as many doctors as she could through Mexico's public healthcare system. She and my father couldn't afford a doctor in private practice; in Mexico, there are two economic classes: the wealthy and the ones who dream of wealth. With the country's free-market system, this division impacts access to quality education, healthcare—everything. The Camacho family was not wealthy. "The doctors were puzzled," my mother has told me. "But I knew something they didn't. I knew there was a little girl waiting to be born. I just had to find someone who could help me."

Remember the dice game—the stubbornness hidden under one of the cups. My mother became pregnant again. This time, fate intervened. A friend said, "There is this doctor I know. He is a friend of the family; he is good. You should go see him."

Dr. Amador was forty-two years old and gifted with an intuitive medical intellect. Such a skilled physician is not easy to find in Mexico. Education, especially higher education, lacks the technology and advanced training common to teaching hospitals in the United States.

My mother heeded Dr. Amador's advice and was bedridden throughout the second half of her pregnancy. At twenty-eight weeks, he prescribed medicine that strengthened both her body and her resolve. For my mother, this pregnancy wound its way down both physical and spiritual paths. Many times, she had the sensation that she had already met this baby, felt the little fingers and toes, and she marveled at the extraordinary life yet to be. Her faith never wavered. Regardless of how poorly she felt or how demanding my brothers Efrain and Salvador were (ages eleven and seven at the time), my mother somehow made her weekly Sunday pilgrimage to our local Catholic church.

Throughout her pregnancy, my mother felt an incredible

connection with God. For the first time in her life, she felt God's presence in her heart. Indeed, our entire family's dynamics changed during that time; everyone focused their energy and prayers on the child my mother was carrying. Even my father, who had never been one to show a lot of emotion or support, helped take care of my brothers, buy groceries, and tend to the house. My brothers pitched in, too. Efrain reflects, "I wanted this baby to be part of our life, and I made up my mind that I would help take care of Mom in extra special ways." So Efrain cleaned and cooked. And he prayed the Hail Mary and the Our Father at night because he knew it would take something bigger than they were to help our mother.

On one particular Sunday, Mass had ended and my mother yearned to stay a bit longer to pray. In one of his new moments of sensitivity, my father agreed to take the boys outside and wait. The church was quiet and still. Light filtered through stained glass windows, and shadows from flickering candles danced along the altar. My mother knelt before Mother Mary, placing her round form before the Virgin's hands, her head covered in black lace. My mother whispered fervent prayers, beseeching God for the little soul inside her.

"God, this is your baby," she said, a hand resting on her belly. "If you give her the opportunity to live, I promise she will be your instrument to do good in this world—" My mother didn't finish her appeal, because at that precise moment, I moved in her womb. To me, this was a direct conversation with God and, on this day, he plainly answered my mother.

Then, the day finally arrived for me to arrive. The complications of my birth—and my survival—defy logic. I was born with the umbilical cord wrapped tightly around my neck, purple and gasping for air. Dr. Amador, accompanied by another doctor, saved me by controlling my breathing and pumping oxygen into my small lungs. (A popular Mexican fable says that people born with their umbilical cord around their necks become very smart! Perhaps the truth is that, for us, life begins with difficulty and pain. We have beaten the odds. Somewhere, deep inside of us, we know this. Our survival instincts have been awakened.)

And, so, my mother's prayers were answered. She was elated. More than that, she was deeply and eternally grateful. I sometimes think I was literally born into the arms of gratefulness. I've never taken my life for granted, and I believe this virtue is the key to happiness. When you are grateful, you look at the world with different eyes. You champion the little things. You leave nothing on the table.

After I was born, my mother hoped for one more child, and she became pregnant again. But as her belly was still growing, Dr. Amador was killed in a terrible car accident. Sadness and despair enveloped my mother's heart—she knew the baby in her womb was at risk, and she didn't know if there would be anyone else to help her. Just as she feared, she began feeling the same symptoms of other pregnancies that had ended in loss. Then, once again, her body was hers alone. My younger sibling died in a miscarriage at four months.

As I grew, there were many nights when my mother took me by the hand as we walked together after dinner. We kicked rocks, swarms of dust flying up from the dirt road. We were happy, making up rhymes and games. One time, she picked up a rock, placed it in my palm, and slowly, carefully, curled my small fingers around it. Her eyes searched my face to make sure her words were forever imprinted in my mind. Even before she spoke, I felt like a superhero being given a mission to save the world from the powers of evil.

"You, Jackie, are like a rock," she said. "Strong, always moving forward, unbreakable. You are not the rock that stands on the side of the river; you are the rock that makes the ripples in the water. You help the river create its own waves. Leave your mark, and remember that strength is inside of you. You entered into this world a fighter. All you have to do is close your eyes and remember who you are and where you came from. Always remember."

My mother calls me a fighter, but she fought for me even before I was born. She believed in me, without reservation or fear, before she ever saw me. She was my first cheerleader and my first mentor, and she is my best friend to this day.

For many years, I wondered, Why me? The circumstances surrounding my birth—my mother's prayers for a little girl, the years of grief, the gentle hands of a skilled physician during a brief window of time—shake me to the core. My takeaway: the world is ours to shape, to ponder, to make better. I am alive. Each day, I look at my life the way a sculptor regards his clay. He envisions the finished piece but is always open to change. He shapes it but, at times, stands back to appreciate the misshapen, awkward work in progress.

In the end, that sculpture is our life story.

## *Fig Factor: Discovery*

Somewhere in the course of life, each of us faces unspeakable struggles. What I have learned from this is that my life is a miracle, given to me by a higher power. I have a successful business, a loving husband, and beautiful children. I've never taken any of it for granted. The choices I've made are born from passion, discipline, and gratitude. These are the essential tools in my life's toolbox. Also, I find great comfort that we are never alone in our life's journey—we have our faith and the love of others around us, just as my mother sought the comfort of God and her family. At the heart of the fig factors lies the belief that our spirituality and belief in others shifts us a little more to the positive, opening us to growing and seeing the world in surprisingly new ways.

When I was much older, my mother told me I was blessed—

that I had an angel watching out for me. Perhaps because I have indeed felt such a presence or because I have dreamed of angels many times, my entire body trembled at her words. As I started to cry, I realized how grateful and humbled I was for the beautiful opportunity to live. Angels walk among us, watching us like silent soldiers, to save, help, protect, guide, and heal us. I believe this as truly as I see a building or tree, solid and sure, or feel the tender touch of my daughter's hand.

As my mother advised, when we remember where we came from, we are better equipped to move forward with courage, unencumbered with disillusionment or uncertainty. When we appreciate the beginning, we discover the key to honoring our life's purpose.

Whenever I stray from my own advice, I take out the rock my mother gave me as a little girl. She was right: I am a fighter. I confess, though, that I never imagined how many times that spirit would be tested!

## Stepping stones to The Fig Factors...

1. When reminiscing about your birth, what do your parents recollect as the most surprising or poignant memory?
2. What is your rock—one item you have that symbolizes strength and courage?

3. Set aside ten minutes in your day to discover life. Think about how you will approach this. Perhaps it will be through taking a long walk or writing a letter. Then listen and watch for what you learn about yourself. Write it down.

4. What are your special gifts or talents? Consider ways to use them more. In so doing, you'll honor your destiny and leave your mark on this world in incredible ways.

5. Look back on your day today. Is there someone who made a difference in your life? Thank them—as soon as possible.

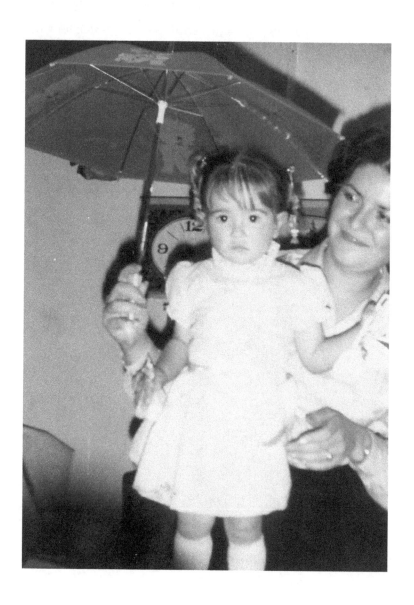

# ② SHARDS OF GLASS

> *"Make others feel important."*
>
> — Dale Carnegie

My first real challenge in life was named Salvador. Seven years my senior, Salvador considered it his vocation to torture his younger sister—me. What he lacked in height, he more than made up for in bravado. He pummeled me with insults, taunting me for my silly ideas and small size, making my life miserable without cause. He chased, and I ran; he pushed, and I cried.

Salvador taught me about fear. As I peeked out from behind my father's shabby, oversized chair, I waited breathlessly in hopes he would pass over my hiding spot. I didn't like the feeling of running away, even if "away" meant the next room. Retreat made me feel small. But confronting a boy twice my height and weight was an intimidating task.

One instance in particular, though, shifted the balance of power ever so slightly—and marked the first time I realized life offered choices rather than mere circumstances. The air was thick with summer heat, made even hotter from my wild dash to escape Salvador's Indian-like war cries. My long black hair whipped around corners as he chased me around the first floor of our house. A lamp tipped over in the living room, and papers from the kitchen counter fluttered like doves to the ground in the wake of our race out the back door and around to the front. I made it inside first, and the thought of locking both the front door and the back door somehow struck my mind. What followed was, to this day, one of my most triumphant moments: I saw my brother standing there, panes of glass separating us. He was powerless.

The realization that strength is often not as important as intellect washed over me in waves. I have used this insight many times in my career. Outsmarting a rival calls for confidence, for planning a sound strategy three levels deep. Something inside me shifted that day; I discovered that being smart offered up steep advantages. From then on, I resolved to learn all I could in life.

In contrast to Salvador, Efrain protected me with a father's hand and heart. He was nearly a dozen years older than I was, and his simple acts of love showed me that the generosity of others sculpts life. He took my hand as though I were a princess and twirled me around in a spontaneous dance amidst giggles and hugs. One time, he gave me a fiery red-orange sunflower clipped from our backyard. *Put this in a little vase on your bureau, because young ladies should always be surrounded by beautiful things.* His tall stature was magnified by the generosity he never failed to show me. He always made me feel important. I would later read books by authors who devoted thousands of pages to this subject, but Efrain was no author. He was simply a person who recognized and honored the value of others as naturally as he took each breath.

During the course of my work, I sometimes share a conference table with people who are rude or impatient or who simply shun the dignity of others. One time, a colleague called me his Latin Lady; another time, a prospective client took up my entire afternoon only to reveal he had no real marketing budget. This is part of life. In those times of frustration or inconvenience, I remember Efrain. For me, he is a placeholder for recognizing the value of others—a reminder to truly see them and not just pass over them in our pursuit of the next opportunity.

By the time I began grade school, my brothers had left to find a better life in the United States, my dad had discovered the elixir of alcohol, and our broken family began a transient lifestyle that would later include me attending three different kindergartens, two different first grades, and two different fourth grades.

My brothers' departure marked first goodbye. Sometimes, the right things to do are the hardest choices to make, and so it was for all of us. Though even I, at that young age, understood that opportunities for education and employment were much greater in the United States, their departure was one of the most difficult times in my life. Even with Salvador! I tell my beautiful children, Leo and Giulianna, that it is hard to live with others, but we all must figure out how to get along, even when our patience is tested and our pride wounded at the hands of our brothers and sisters.

The day Efrain and Salvador left, I clutched them on our front walk until they had to pull away. Then I ran—not away from something this time, but toward emotions I had never before understood: grief, loss, and sadness. Hot tears dampened the white tissues strewn throughout my room. I could not sit and accept; I moved around like a wounded bird, searching desperately for flight. In my frantic pacing, the vase that had once held that beautiful red-orange ray of sunshine smashed to the floor. Light falls differently for all of us in our lives. All I saw, startled from the crash, were the shadows clutching the edges of those glass pieces. *Adios, mi hermanos, te quiero.*

For days on end after that, my father was simply gone. In fact, on the days he was with us, I don't remember him not drinking. A fistful of seasons suddenly became years, over which my dad gradually crossed the line from social drinking to addiction. He didn't realize his steps were taking him farther and farther away from me, but once again, fear was a frequent companion in both my dreams and waking hours. The invisible threat that one day my father would never return darkened our days like a constant rain. What if an accident claimed his life? What if someone else was hurt because of his carelessness? *What did I do to drive him away?* It is amazing how the sounds of night are different when you have lost the daily presence of a father. Everything is amplified and exaggerated. A passing car seems treacherous and invasive. Small sounds become the careless markings of an intruder. My old life was a remnant now, a part of something that I would never fully get back.

And, so, I sought the refuge of words. The knowledge books gave me was dependable and unchanging, a constant pillar during years when we moved from home to home within the expanse of Mexico City.

I began reading when I was four years old. My cousin reminds me of my love of words whenever we reminisce about our youth. She said my reading at such a young age fascinated her. If my hands could reach it, I read it: labels on cans of food, brochures, tissue boxes, and maps. Curiosity propelled me to collect knowledge like beach shells. The more I read, the more I thought, *I could write like that.* The more I saw, the more *I thought, I could figure out how to do that.* These were the mind games of a child. I had tasted the concept of challenge and found it utterly delicious.

With my father's frequent absences, my mother had to find a way to support the two of us. It was hard, but reading books gave me peace and certainty that there was a better future. They were my escape from reality into an amazing world of possibility. I imagined a stable home, unfettered by financial or family worries. I envisioned myself dressed in clothes like those my mom wore, earning money by doing interesting things in business. The stories I read in books were about successful people, and they filled my head with untethered dreams. I imagined what it would feel like to experience that kind of success—of having the things I wanted without concern for money and using my resources to make a difference in the lives of others. What if I could break the barriers and achieve true success in life? What if I could find my life's passion and exercise it every day while making money and helping others? A day has never gone by without doing something, whether small or large, that gets me closer to this vision. These questions nip at my heels like a faithful dog.

While a transient life left me yearning for a permanent home, the experience cultivated my ability to adapt. Friends came and went. Neighborhoods changed. But one thing remained: I could pick up a book and feel empowered. My mom valued education even though she had little of it. Perhaps this made her even more vigilant that I continue learning. She fueled my curiosity by exposing me to every event, book, and person she could find with lessons to teach, and she constantly assured me that I was destined to achieve greatness. She challenged me to figure out how I could have handled situations better with others and encouraged me to ask questions when I didn't have the answers. I took her advice, and an insatiable pursuit of knowledge carried over into becoming a straight-A student.

Not only did I feel accomplished by conquering subjects like math, language, and science, I happily shared my love of learning with others. When I was in second grade, I supplied a neighbor friend with nearly flawless homework assignments daily. She was three grades ahead of me in school. It never occurred to me that this was unusual. And it definitely never occurred to me that it was wrong! With every school I attended, I absorbed information. I may never have seen the math problems before, but I did them because I believed anything was possible. They were puzzles, and all puzzles have solutions. I could solve any of them.

In tandem with my mother's pursuit to better our family's situation, my father's drinking also progressed, creating a two-steps-forward, one-step-back sputter to our lives. I do believe he wanted to be a better father and husband, but he was overwhelmed by his own problems. So, when my grandmother offered us property in Malpaso, a small town seven hours from Mexico City where my dad was born, the idea of moving seemed like an opportunity for a man perhaps hoping for a second chance.

"My father, he died when I was young. I was so little," he would say with a pinched look to his sun-bronzed face. Then he would describe the town and I dreamed that I had lived there, too. "We were soldiers on the hills armed with stick guns and trees as our guard towers. There was so much open land around our village. As a young boy, I could do anything in my little town. I was happy. And then, suddenly, my dad was gone. Stomach cancer. Funny how you can hold someone's hand one day and then never hold it again. No doctors could help him. He was only thirty years old. An uncle took me in. I was one less mouth to feed out of six. I moved to the city when I was seven and always looked back with regret and resentment."

Can a place define who we are? Who we might become? In my dad's eyes, Malpaso created hope for a new start. He shared his drawings and plans for our new house, smoothing out the large blueprints on the kitchen table as carefully as though they were sheets of glass. Those prints reflected a new life for my dad, showing me just how much he craved peace, simultaneously sought for and barred by his addiction. Like many children of alcoholics, I do not drink, and I consider my choice a gift from my dad.

The first time I saw Malpaso, Calvillo, in the State of Aguascalientes, my seven-year-old heart leapt for joy. Cobblestone streets, aged churches, and patchwork squares of textured yellow and green farms welcomed me. We arrived in a pale blue 1974 Impala outlined in rust. I carefully used the hand crank to lower the window and drank in the sights, the smells, the tapestry of what lay before me. I was ready to find my place within this new world.

Many of the six thousand people who lived there were wealthy, benefitting from the region's abundant fruit: guava. Without such resources, my father built the walls of our house with intuition and strategic thinking. He was amazing, developing the architectural plans without any formal training. He was an agent who worked on and off with celebrities appearing on Televisa, the country's largest television station. I know, in my quietist moments, that he inspired in me a desire to reach the top of every mountain. His repeated attempts at business spoke volumes on not giving up. I part ways, however, in how alcohol usurped my father's line of sight for what was most important: his family. It led my father to choose a different path that veered far beyond Malpaso.

The last room of the house to be completed was on the second floor. It was to be done soon after we moved in. Today, twenty years later, the plaster in that room remains unfinished, electrical wires hanging like frustrated hands amidst a patchy white ceiling. The money my father should have used to finish the house disappeared. My parents constantly argued about this and so many other things. I can still hear the screams of my father, calls of frustration and resentment against a life he didn't know he had—a beautiful wife, a daughter who adored him, a house that he could have made a home, two sons who would have been there had their father he made different choices. Instead, the smell of gin and beer hung heavy in the air when we were together, a pile of empty bottles left behind when he was gone. All he had to do was love us and take care of us. To a young girl, this seems simple, but for a man in the clutches of his personal demons, it is far from easy. *Efrain, I need you. Do you remember me? Where are your beautiful green eyes to comfort me and tell me everything will be all right? If only for a moment, I need you.*

I close my eyes and think about that unfinished room. When the people in our lives play second to things, we all leave a room unfinished inside us. Fame is fleeting, money is accessible, power is a myth, but people—they are the light that guides our way.

My hopes and dreams were quickly crushed when we entered that little town. I never belonged. Townsfolk had spent generations there; we were never welcomed. People walking by just continued walking. I was rarely invited to go to parties or join friends. Early on, I dreamed about going back to Mexico City to achieve my dreams of becoming a recognized success in some way. The big city life shone more brilliantly now that I was away.

School was my haven. I loved school because it constantly challenged, judged, and rewarded me—even if it was only with a good grade. I gathered accomplishments, both little and big, like pebbles in my hand. They would build a platform that allowed me to become an entrepreneur someday. Yes, some day.

My aspirations contrasted with the smallness of thought that seemed to me to be everywhere. Bullies criticized the way

I talked; they resented my intelligence and rejected my efforts to become friends. I was falsely labeled the "rich girl from the city." No one could go anywhere without the entire town knowing and gossiping about the places where you might have been before. Truth held no regard in those conversations.

On one occasion, the neighbor kids were all playing stickball outside. Moms and dads sat on front porches under a beautiful early evening sky. As I passed by on my bike, many of the kids hurled names and rude comments at me. Zorrai, they called to me. A play on my middle name, Saray, the word meant "fox" in Spanish, with a far different connotation than the same slang in English. Crushed, I felt the movement of my bike but froze from the coldness of their words. Their judgment was asphyxiating. For a long time, I tried to adapt. I am not sure I ever did. I did, however, learn the value of inclusivity by living its opposite.

More alone than ever before, my mother and I made a silent pact. In the absence of the people who should have played a prominent role in our lives—my father for my mom and friends for me—we marched forward together and created a better life for both of us.

My childhood days of kicking rocks and making up rhymes with my mother were now replaced with staying by her side through all her meetings and business presentations. My mother was a saleswoman, and I was awestruck by everything she did.

She took me with her everywhere—whether she was selling cosmetics or nutritional supplements or food. I saw her clients' homes. I attended corporate meetings. I missed nothing.

We visited many wealthy people's homes, and I always dreamed about living in such grand houses with beautiful tapestries, terrazzo-tiled floors, and elegant furniture. Manicured gardens and pools made me feel as though I were visiting a rock star's home. I questioned why we did not have such things but somehow knew in my heart that if I worked consistently hard, like my mom, I would make it happen. I loved seeing her provide solutions to her clients and get results. There was a sense of pride and happiness every time someone said "Thank you," or "This was wonderful for me." I dreamed of the day when I would do my own selling. I wanted to help as many people as possible, too.

My mother's attire was simple yet stunning. We could not afford many things—sometimes it took an entire year just to save for a pair of shoes—but she believed that quality trumped quantity. At first glance, her closet was never full, but with accessories like scarves and belts, she made a suit look completely different with every wearing. She told me how important it was to "dress to impress." I idolized her. Her perfume lingers in my memory even now, and I feel her soft, reassuring hand wrapped around mine. She worked so hard to get sales, waking early each day and making sure she was always on time for each appointment.

As I got older, I started helping her. While I had my share of teenage tantrums outside of "work," I never failed to put all of my energy into helping her win as many sales as possible. We sold Jafra, a line of upscale, natural makeup and skincare products, and eventually Herbalife brand nutritional supplements. I accompanied my mom on demonstrations and often made the presentation myself with my mom's guidance. I was so proud that my neat handwriting earned me the privilege of helping her prepare orders. Since my mom's formal education only extended to second grade, both my writing and math skills came in handy. I followed up with clients by phone and offered them advice under my mom's supervision, motivating them to buy more products. It was fun. We won trips, saw celebrities, earned VIP tickets to events, and made extra money to buy shoes or clothes. People were fascinated by my business acumen at this tender age. Many of her clients enjoyed my youthful enthusiasm, and I quickly gained their respect and a reputation of being "smart" beyond my years.

Recently, a friend was telling me how she remembers that I was never afraid to talk with people, and I was always curious. My friend remembered how my mom empowered me, wanting me to expand on her own dreams of a financially independent lifestyle, a confident and self-assured attitude, and business success in whatever field I chose. In the end, she wanted me to have a happier life, but she also wanted me to be the one to create it without complete dependence on a husband. In my eyes, my mom made things happen as much as she could. As a mother now, I see that the world we show our children is indeed the world that shapes who they are.

Besides the insatiable desire to achieve, my mom gave me another rare gift: the books that would become my literary mainstay. Reading so young allowed me to devour great literature by authors like Dale Carnegie, Napoleon Hill, Zig Ziglar, and Og Mandino. "All the success you will ever achieve will be in direct proportion to how many people you help become successful," whispered the pages authored by Mr. Ziglar. And from Mr. Carnegie I learned to "make others feel important." Rhonda Bryne taught me "all the answers are inside of you." Napoleon Hill opened up possibilities with "whatever your mind can conceive, you can achieve."

Later, when I came to America, I would have gladly left any of my belongings behind with the exception of those worn, treasured books. Wisdom comes from the voices of those who have tried, failed, and tried again. Being surrounded by these great writers connected me with a body of knowledge that honed my ambitions and crafted my business skills. I analyzed them as if I were going to teach a course on their principles. My mother, too, was enamored with self-help books, memoirs of accomplished people, and sales-building advice from top experts. She also loved poetry and wrote a collection of beautiful poems to us as children.

All these voices echoing in my head encouraged me to imagine the possibilities. I was awake!

The rumblings inside me nurtured a strong desire to be something greater than what I was and to help others feel the same way, especially on the days my mother felt defeated. Defeat is an interesting notion to reconcile for one who seemed so invincible. Yes, one day, she was motivated and ready to take on the world, and the next week she was overwhelmed from the fallout of my dad's drinking and our financial pressures. Again, her faith guided her. She felt close to God and prayed often during difficult times. She would say, *We are a small family, and it does not make sense to be separated. We must be united. One day, we will all be together again,* meaning my two brothers, my dad, and the two of us. Her dream, in part, was realized because my brothers and I are now very close. Our bonds today grew from the love and the importance of family she showed us.

In the quiet of my mother's fears, my strength rose up and embraced the woman I idolized. She is the single greatest influence in making me want to take on new challenges. While other girls my age were concerned with their looks or a boyfriend, I felt a strange, burning desire to singlehandedly change the world.

That is not to say that I was always modest. Being the only girl and the youngest, I sometimes thought I was the most important person in the world. I was top of my class in every school I went to and won many races as a runner in school. I enjoyed the spotlight. But children thrive in self-centeredness; their innocence offers up a narrow view that is completely forgiven in their development of self-worth. When adults possess the same trait, they are not as easily forgiven. In the end, I discovered as I got older that it is far better to focus on others than myself. Sharing a kind word of encouragement and truly listening when people share their stories offers great rewards.

Looking back at my youth, I realize that the secret to what one will become is often revealed during our early years. I was always putting on talent shows and hosting contests. It seemed as though hundreds of kids—it probably was more like dozens— were at my house. I made posters advertising all sorts of events; I rallied others to do things. I yearned to wear suits every day. I wanted to answer the phone and be the voice connecting people to opportunities.

The truth is that children do the things they love, which is why they don't clean their rooms, dust, vacuum, or do laundry. Children know something we adults leave behind. They unhesitatingly take up activities that feed their souls, give them joy, and accentuate their God-given talents. Without trying, they are wise.

Wisdom is a funny thing. While this virtue may be predicated on knowledge, sometimes the smartest person in the room can make unwise choices. Why? Because they cannot see the big picture and the precious people who are in it. Or they stop assessing who they are and get stuck in momentary struggles. All those books, all those experiences, created in me a wisdom so vibrant it shaped my vision—a dream, really—that grew in rhythm with the days. I remember thinking I was in a little town, but I wasn't going to stay there; I was going to get out some day and do amazing things.

I was fourteen years old when my opportunity came, purely by chance...

# Fig Factor: Wisdom

Wisdom is a word deserving of a second look. By definition, it is comprised of three parts: knowledge, insight, and . . . judgment. Wisdom, then, is the judicious use of the lessons we learn. Each day we are given a clean sheet of paper on which we can rewrite our story with the wisdom we gather through our experiences and relationships, our failures and successes. So, grab your piece of paper and run with it.

### Stepping stones to The Fig Factors . . .

1. What three books have influenced you? In what ways?
2. How would you define the word wisdom, and how do you apply this in your life?

3. What the three values (i.e., courage, wisdom, integrity, etc.) are most important to you?

4. How do you bring those values to life?

5. What activities did you like as a child? Are they still a part of your life? If not, how can you reconnect with them?

# PART TWO:
*With Growth, a Plant Emerges*

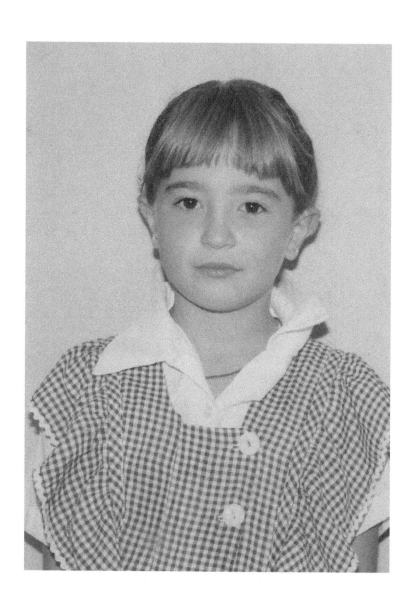

## 3

# FIRE, FIRE!

*"You can have everything in life you want, if you will just help other people get what they want."*

— Zig Ziglar

One particular memory of Malpaso will forever be colored black. Not the velvet, sumptuous black of night or the strong, reaffirming black of iron, but the black left behind from a blaze that nearly consumed our home—and, along with that, a handful of my innocence.

A menagerie of people move in a slow, rhythmic mist of memory: old ones cloaked in shriveled skin and drinking Fanta orange pop, widows dressed forever now in death's color, young men showcasing their bravado in white muscle shirts and tight jeans, children playing . . .

I was one of those children, just ten years old, the day my world changed. *Tag, you're it. Rock, paper, scissors. Kick the ball to me, I'm open.* About twenty of us played in the plaza that warm June evening. My mom was selling tacos in a small stand nearby.

Suddenly, smoke overcame the air from afar. Voices turned

toward me, coming from blurry faces—like the people we meet between sleep and wakefulness.

The scene was no dream, however. *Fuego, fuego! Tu casa!*

There, at the highest point of Malpaso, sat my home, engulfed in flames. Not by a chance match or a forgotten candle. Instead, it was a fire fueled by envy.

As I saw in school soon after we first arrived in Malpaso, many of the small-minded people in that tiny town thought we were wealthy. *The Camacho family, they're from the big city. Big shots. They're different. The mother dresses like she's a princesa. The girl, she reads. Books all over their house. No girl is good enough for those boys.*

In truth, we were a middle class family scratching out a life. And while my grandma hailed from Malpaso and raised her children there, my dad was forced to move to the big city. To the locals, we were traitors of sorts, our roots tentative, and that was a point of contention with many of them. The label they forced on us inspired an act of treachery.

Mom held my hand as we walked home, and we cried in disbelief the entire way. The smell of smoke, unlike anything I had ever experienced, gained strength with every step. We walked quickly. People approached us, offering their condolences and gestures of help. *What would we need? Would we have a home? Would everything be gone?* We were the center of attention, but not in a way I had ever hoped.

As we watched, our faces flushed red from the heat of the flames and our hearts rigid with fear, we held each other close. Our brick home stood before us like a giant oven, its contents burning mercilessly inside: toys, furniture, books, and glass décor we would never touch again. Plates, games, couches, clothes, jewelry—the things we had worked for and loved were gone. Salvador had saved and worked for a year to buy a set of speakers that now lay in a heap of ash. The beautiful set of encyclopedias we had saved our money to buy would never be used again.

Author Salman Rushdie once said that the story you finish is never the one you begin. The fire, as horrible as it was, introduced me to compassion, community, and gratitude. My story had taken a decidedly new turn that laid a foundation of positivity in the face of adversity for the remainder of my life.

People in the town, despite their differences with our family, came running from their houses with sloshing buckets of water in hand. Small towns in Mexico didn't have fire stations, and Malpaso was no exception. My family stood before the flames watching dozens of people trying desperately to help. Maria, the owner of a small grocery store across the street, passed buckets. Josefina, the nosey neighbor who lived directly across from our house, brought water from her home. The town sheriff turned water on and off. Old people with snowy white hair, barefoot children, and people dressed nicely from work all came to our rescue. They stopped what they were doing to help us without question or reward. Their empathy comforted me in some small way—just knowing we shared our sadness with others made that sadness slightly more bearable.

Hours passed like years; the flames slowly receded and a harsh reality took their place. We walked carefully inside the house. Amidst the despair, we were grateful that no one was harmed. We wanted to be there surrounded by the wreckage while wishing we were a thousand miles away. I tripped over debris. Was it the crocheted pillow my grandmother made me? *Abuela, why has this happened to us?* My small hands reached out to pick up my favorite doll. It was the one Claudia, my best friend, had given me the night before we left Mexico City. The figure disintegrated under my touch, the plastic string still hot to the touch. Gone.

My room, my home, the table we ate dinner at, the chair my father sat in, the pretty clothes my mother wore, my school books, the window I looked out from when I talked to the stars, my home—gone. My mom was devastated, but she said something I will never forget: *We are okay.* I think about this now, and the image that appears in my mind is that of a tree. Trees grow faster and stronger in a storm, their roots clutching deep within the earth with every pull and tug of the wind. They fight to stay, and that is when their roots grow longer, deeper, fuller. The fire caused my roots to grow that night and all the sad days that followed. And my mother's words made me realize this: *Everything will be okay.* I began to believe.

No more poignant moment occurred that night, however, than when I discovered nearly all my books had left me. Their ashes fell like sand from my fingers. We found out later that the fire must have started near my beloved books, lined up like soldiers on what was the most important part of the house to me: a bookshelf ten feet long and eight feet high directly under the vacant opening to the upper floor left unfinished by my father. As I crouched down and touched those ruined pages, I decided that knowledge was something no one could ever take away from me. I read those books; they would be inside me for the rest of my life. No fire or person could steal inner knowledge from me. Now, it was up to me to apply those principles and use them to help others and achieve my dreams.

For the next two months, we lived in an adjacent house, a one-room structure that had belonged to my uncle before he passed away. It was tiny and cold and ugly. We lived there with little privacy or joy. But it made me grateful for our real home and was a constant reminder of what we had lost. For a long time, nightmares plagued my sleep. Sometimes I dreamed that I was in the fire with no way out. I could see all the people I loved on the other side, but there was no way to reach them. Flames separated us, flames that never seemed to go away but remained yellow-orange and terrifying until I awoke to the relief that there was no fire and I, like my mother had said, would be okay.

Months later, I still found ash on my school uniform. Every

time I washed my hair, remnants of black ashes fell upon me. I don't know where it came from, but it was a constant reminder of what happened. Students at the Catholic school I attended pointed and made fun of me. I was in class one day wearing my checkered blue uniform, and I looked down at my skirt to see it smeared with black marks. I wondered if the fire would ever really be over or if I would have to endure ash marks the rest of my life. Tears flowed, and I realized I would need to choose to move on, with or without those black marks.

The last thing I recall about the fire resonates with me even now. We never wanted to know who did it. My father chose not to know. *To put a face to this devastation, Jackie, would be more heartbreaking than the fire itself.*

In the smallest of decisions comes the greatest of lessons. What my father was trying to do was focus on the good. The good of the people who helped us that fateful night. The good that no one was hurt. The good of our family's triumph over tragedy.

*Thank you, Papa.* Finding the good in others was the one big lesson my dad gave me, which makes it even more precious. I would steel myself with this in the days ahead as I faced a new country with a language I did not understand, a pace that often left me frustrated, and a youth culture foreign to even my wildest dreams

# *Fig Factor: Humility*

The heat of the flames still haunts me. I cry sometimes when I think of that night. But the generosity of the people who helped warms my heart and extinguishes the loss. Stepping back and taking in the love and care of other people is a humbling feeling. People often confuse humility for weakness. It is quite the opposite. Strong people accept the help of others and recognize the human spirit for what it truly is: the heart's way of sharing.

**Stepping stones to The Fig Factors . . .**

1. Consider a time when someone took you from disappointment to gratitude. How did that person change your perspective?
2. Choose an article from a newspaper or magazine that highlights a crisis. Now . . . find the good in the story.
3. What small things can you do to make a difference in someone else's life today? This month? This year?
4. Is it difficult or easy for you to accept help from others? Why?

## 4

# NEW COUNTRY, NEW LIFE

*"Whatever your mind can conceive, you can achieve."*

— Napoleon Hill

In dreams, I felt myself running swiftly. However, regardless of my urging forward, my stance remained rooted in one spot with the scenes of my life passing me as jagged, stilted frames in an old black and white movie. I saw the streets of Mexico with books stacked to the sky and the stone houses of Malpaso hovering above flames and billows of smoke. *Run harder, Jackie, run faster, time steals days that later become years.* Kids from my town stood silently in open green-yellow fields with patches of brown earth, their postures eerily statuesque as they watched me turn toward things that weren't there. *Look forward, see your destination, discover your stride.*

I awoke from those dreams a fourteen-year-old girl with arms wrapped tight around soft white sheets and a pink coverlet. I knew those dreams revealed a longing for something other than what I had. My life's journey, a tangle of triumph over disappointment, had nurtured a desire to leave Malpaso and explore new possibilities. I yearned to realize the last scene in my dream: my destination.

As a teenager, I continued to excel academically. Still, I felt unfulfilled. The audience that had attended the talent shows and parades of my ponytailed childhood days was gone. My efforts toward excellence remained unnoticed by classmates, teachers, and the culture in which I lived. Years after moving to the United States, I would attend an art reception and see a piece that beautifully captured my feelings while living in Malpaso. The painting, entitled *Lucha por la Libertad*, or Fight for Liberty, was created by a young artist named Juan Sepulveda. It reminded me of Mexico's biggest challenge: the small-mindedness and competitive nature of its people. The painter, born and raised in Mexico, represented the country through a vintage Mexican army general wearing the rich colors and poignant mottos of our various political parties, including one leg half consumed by tarantulas. The dangerous and prolific spiders, which are considered the scourge of our country, represented the warring factions that the artist believed held our beautiful nation back from real progress. Nationally, there have been few instances when our people worked together toward the same goal. Instead, every man has long stood for himself alone.

This was how I felt in Malpaso. Many from our town preyed on the weaknesses of others, concerned only about their own lives.

People seemed to ignore the good in their neighbors. When it came time to recognize another's accomplishments, their tongues remained silent. On one particular day, I rushed to my paternal grandmother's house, so excited to show her my report card. My joy melted away under her cold voice, pursed lips, and attitude of "So what?" I picked up the pieces of my pride, carefully put my report card back in its envelope, and walked slowly home. For a long time after, though, I automatically connected the experience of never being good enough with going the extra mile. Memory's ink fades slowly on a young mind. Run, Jackie, see the world of possibilities, the voice of my dreams whispered to me.

Run... where? Life spun out of control financially as my father's neglect left us relying on our own resourcefulness and my brothers' support. Efrain and Salvador's departure continued to leave me feeling fractured. My heart felt bruised by the broken pieces of our family strewn across faraway places. Phone calls were too costly for us to initiate from Mexico, so each month I waited anxiously to hear the phone ring, their voices on the other end. They lived in a remote world I could barely picture— an apartment shared with several friends, where they had comfortable beds and plenty of food to eat. The warmth of their love contrasted with the loneliness welling deep within me as we said our goodbyes at the end of those calls. But, while hundreds of miles separated us, they taught me something I will never forget. They said *Jackie, productivity equals time, and time equals money.*

Efrain's sixty-plus-hour workweek consisted of two restaurant jobs, and Salvador, too, worked at a restaurant, eventually moving on to a car dealership. My brothers sent us money regularly, but the financial support did not make up for the emotional void of their absence. My mom felt the fractures most deeply. She remembered the little boys with dirt-smudged faces and a blanket of clothes on their bedroom floors—what she would have given to tousle their hair or make their lunch again. The pictures of my brothers, a red racecar left behind, a plastic toy soldier... these things meant something to a mother who loved her children. She needed her family together as it had once been, and she was determined to make it happen.

My mother began making plans to reunite us by moving to the United States. The immensity of this decision fell upon my dad like the unexpected swipe of a hammer's head. He had been to California once, years ago, and had not liked the United States—the fast pace, the constant rush and pressure of time. He loved Malpaso, this small, sleepy town surrounded by nature, where no step was quickened with a sense of urgency. He didn't want to go, but he wanted to be estranged from his family even less.

One day, in a rare moment when he was home, he asked me, "Do you want to go to the United States, Jackie?"

I looked at him seriously. "Dad, I want that more than anything else in the whole world. If I stay here, I'm going to marry our neighbor, have ten children, and that's going to be the end of the story. I want to change the world, but I need a platform; I need people who appreciate progress and a new environment to explore the possibilities."

He confided in me years later that our conversation was a deciding factor in his choice to come to the United States. He saw the hope in my eyes, the sincerity of my spirit, and the desire to fulfill a vocation unreachable had I stayed in Malpaso.

The same innocent, raw hope he saw color my eyes is no different from the hope I see in people's eyes today. People from all walks of life search, hope, and dream: college graduates, individuals reinventing themselves mid-life, women searching for their new role within hardworking families, entrepreneurs on the path to success, and those struggling to make payroll. My dad saw this, my mother honored it, and, suddenly we were driving northwest toward a state graphic with mountains. I counted the hours on a sheet of paper just to make the time go by faster until finally the landscape changed. Forests played hopscotch with cities, and everything smelled clean. I also saw something I had read about but never seen: snow-capped mountains. Even from a distance, they were magnificent. In less than a week, we had arrived in Colorado, where one of my uncles lived. It was 1997, and the United States had just celebrated its birthday. Efrain drove from Chicago to meet us. I still see him in my mind's eye: his complexion was lighter from the lack of sunlight we are exposed to all the time in Mexico, and he walked confidently, head held high, shoulders back. My brother looked . . . important, as if he had been to a special place and done meaningful things. Efrain had made his way in the world on his own. The reunion overflowed with love. Just thinking about the emotion that day gives me goose bumps. My brother, the one who had always protected me as a little girl, once again came to our aid. He gave me a good, long hug, surrounding me with the solid warmth of his arms. I was home.

* * *

For the first seven months, we all lived in a one-bedroom apartment in Hoffman Estates, a small suburb northwest of Chicago. It was wonderful to be together again, but our new home was tight. My bedroom was a walk-in closet, my bed a greenish gray sleeping bag. It was less than I'd had before, but it was a safe place where I could bury my head as I listened to my parents' angry voices spit out words in Spanish. My brothers slept on the living room couches, seemingly unaware of my parents' arguments, or so it seemed to a girl who *felt* everything around her.

Outside our apartment, my new world shocked my senses. Why couldn't we just walk to places? Why did we need a credit card? How could there be more stores than people? The sheer speed with which people worked and lived in the United States made my head spin. And the culture! People dressed so casually, while in Mexico, even with little money to spend, we dressed nicely each day regardless of our plans. People in the United States seemed not to care how they looked on a daily basis, and I remember thinking that wasn't such a bad thing. They were going places, seeing things, learning, and they did it sans a dress code. The environment fascinated me. People had options and priorities that were so different from ours; our family was just trying to survive. Would I ever be in a position to make choices? *Go out to dinner or stay home? Get my hair cut or do my nails?* The possibility felt remote when, as the frostbitten Illinois winter approached, we did not even have proper clothes. I often wore my brothers' huge jackets over my lighter summer blouses and skirts to block the cutting wind.

These realities—finding clothes that fit or putting food on the table—didn't seem to exist for many people. Every time I visited an American friend's house, it seemed as though food was abundant—cookies and bread in the pantry, the refrigerator packed with fruit, and cans of pop in a second refrigerator. *I thought, If I only had all the fruit I wanted!* Even now, I privately celebrate the bounty in my kitchen.

Despite the worries, my blessings were abundant. Many people leave their homeland because they have little hope for getting ahead there. They dream of unlimited possibilities and better lives for their children In America. Soon, however, survival displaces the American dream. Children sacrifice education to make money for their families. The same fate would have befallen me if not for my brothers. For all the trouble Salvador gave me as a child, he had become a caring, selfless brother who, along with Efrain, would always be a hero in my eyes. They worked so my parents could pay our bills without requiring me to get a job. Because of their devotion to our family, I was able to focus on my schoolwork.

While I had been a strong student in Mexico, I now faced the biggest challenge of my life: being an immigrant who did not speak the language. I entered Schaumburg High School as a freshman. The student body was mostly Caucasians, making it more difficult to succeed but also pushing me to learn faster. On my first day, a nice woman in a purple suit and high heels informed me that it was going to take four years for me to understand English fully. She told me that as a freshman, I would study English as a second language; as a sophomore, I would be enrolled in the intermediate level; as a junior, in the advanced level; and, finally, as a senior, I would be bilingual.

*Sorry,* I thought, *but no.* I had spent a lifetime waiting to walk these halls. How could I wait three or four years to be bilingual, to share my dreams, to help others, to be normal? Words were inside me, English words. I had to let them out—so I immediately got to work.

What began as a game quickly became my most important tool in learning English. I challenged myself to remove a random word in an ad or billboard and write it down in a special journal. If I saw the word on multiple signs, then I knew it was important to learn. For example, I would take the word "nice" and write it ten to twenty times. I may not have known how to say it, what it meant, or how to use it, but I knew that writing it was a crucial step, especially in English, a language in which words are not always pronounced the same way they are written. I paid special attention to words that were used repeatedly. Americans love long sentences. Conjunctions like "but," "and," and "or" stitched thoughts together in print and in people's speech. Pronouns were ubiquitous, and articles, while not very interesting, were in nearly every sentence. One word I saw frequently was "free," an oxymoron, as nothing seemed to be free here. When I learned every meaning of the word I was studying, I applied each definition to the sign or billboard or news article to see which was accurate, and whether removing the word changed the essence of the sentence's original meaning. My formula for learning the meanings of words worked! Just as I devoured puzzles as a child, the more I discovered, the more I wanted to learn.

I remember the day I realized I was bilingual. I woke up one morning after having a dream—in English. How different this dream was from all those I had experienced in Mexico! There, I stood still, watching life pass me by. Here, I was flying forward with vivid clarity. And I was doing it while speaking English.

Within my first year at Schaumburg High School, my teacher observed my progress and put me in a normal curriculum. One of the first courses was American Studies. Amidst a class discussion one day, I accidentally used the word "bean" instead of "being." I didn't know the difference; I thought it meant the same thing. "Bean!" my classmates laughed. "Listen to that, what a beaner!"

My face flushed; I was mortified. Though I didn't understand what I'd done wrong, I knew they were making fun of me. "Beaner" became my new nickname, and classmates excluded me from group activities. Lunchtime was a gauntlet of snickers and whispered comments as I tried to find a place to sit. At times, I wondered why I hadn't stuck to the four-year ESL program. Why had I been so demanding with myself, trying to learn the language so quickly? Maybe if I had conformed to the system, I wouldn't feel like such an outcast. The experience was devastating—and it all stemmed from mispronouncing one small word.

Outside of school, I found comfort in Mrs. Magdalena Morales. I will never forget her kindness and support when we arrived. A friend from church introduced us. Mrs. Morales was ancient, proud, and loving. She admired our desire to improve our lives. At times, I felt like she understood me in ways others did not. She saw past my teenage angst and encouraged me to succeed in school and in life. Little moments became memorable with Mrs. Morales. No matter what we were doing, we stopped and visited when she came by. She would ask, "How are you doing, Jackie? Do you have everything you need for school?" She drove my mom and me to church or different events, even if it meant driving completely out of her way and getting home late. She took us to Christmas celebrations with Mexican-themed posadas to help us make peace with our homesickness. There were times I couldn't understand why she did so much for us when we had nothing to give her in return.

Despite my longing to leave one place for another, I missed the familiarity of the things that had surrounded me when I was younger. Even the taste of food—the *same* food—was so different. Hamburgers in Mexico were more flavorful than the ones here. Mom's recipes did not taste quite the same even with the same ingredients—that was, if she could even find all the ingredients. Often, one or two key spices couldn't be found in the grocery stores, and the same meals tasted flat and unfamiliar.

I lived in conflicting worlds: I didn't want to go back to Mexico, but I also felt like a stranger ready to run at the first chance. I needed to embrace something, but I wasn't quite sure what it was or how I would do this. I missed my familiar surroundings in Malpaso and the simplicity of life there, even though it was laced with envy and frustration. I was enthralled by the possibilities here in the United States, but I was still held back by my differences.

During those teenage years, my mom and brothers tried to help me understand their sacrifices that allowed me to stay in school. Salvador would throw my sweatshirt at my feet, exasperated at my stubbornness, and point out that all I had to do was study while he worked to help pay the rent. My mom bit back frustration as I slammed doors and offered up one-word answers. It's hard to look outside yourself at that age. Some days, I felt so vacant and unappreciative because of the other kids' scorn. I did not know who I was, I was embarrassed at school, and I brought my frustration home right along with my books and homework. It was not fair to the people I loved, but I had no idea how to deal with all those emotions..

During this time, my mom's patience and love were always there for me. An amazing singer, she delighted us with her beautiful voice as she made food or cleaned the house. In quiet moments between meetings and a busy family life, I listen for my mother's sweet voice and recall the time when I was forced to grow as a person and find my way.

Of course, my mother struggled with the transition as much as anyone. The first winter we spent in the United States, my mom stood by the window after she arrived home from work. Tears rolled down her cheeks.

I touched her shoulder with alarm. "Mom, what's wrong?"

In between quiet sobs, she said, "How could this be possible? I went to work when it was completely dark and I came home and it is completely dark... Where are my days?"

Where were our days? Everything was different. It was not easy to find joy in the cold weather or the fact that we did not have a lot of money—but the simple fact that we were together as a family and did not have to experience the scrutiny of our neighbors kept us going.

One of the best things to come from our move was that my dad stopped drinking. Perhaps he thought it was a way to make up for past mistakes. As an adult, I recognize his strong will and yearning for us to be together; I realize how difficult sobriety must have been for him. Indeed, it was the most important sacrifice I witnessed from my father, but I didn't fully understand it back then. Alcohol was an elixir whose siren call he constantly struggled to resist, and there were days he shook uncontrollably with the effort. Sometimes he burst with frustration, snapping at insignificant things like a door left open or my backpack in the way. I was never scared he would hurt us, but I often fought panic that he wouldn't take care of us. I channeled that energy back into school.

As my American Studies class was readying for a speech on the American Revolution, I decided that I was not about to be embarrassed again. I practiced my speech to everyone who would listen—my brothers, the janitors, my teachers, even my teddy bears. The day of my speech, I stood in front of the class, shaking and trying to control my breathing. The "bean" debacle taunted me—but I was ready. Accolades from previous speeches I had done in Spanish flooded back to me. I wanted to taste that sweet recognition again.

I delivered the speech exactly as I had practiced. I paused when I needed to accentuate a point and made eye contact with everyone I could, never needing to glance down at my eight typed pages. I was completely and wholly in the moment, not even realizing I was speaking English but reveling in the feeling that I was achieving something important. When it was over and I floated back to my seat, I felt alive, accomplished, and complete.

"Excellent job, Jackie," my teacher said, smiling. Several of my classmates nodded and smiled, leaning over to tell me which parts they liked best. All the emotion I had held at bay while preparing for the speech gave way, and relief swept over me. I fought tears of happiness. I had nailed it—I just knew it!

Sure enough, only one other student earned an A, and I received an A+. Suddenly, people accepted me. I was invited to sit at classmates' lunch tables and was included in group activities. *Sweet victory, Jackie—you did it.*

While the glory of that turnaround day was wonderful, I had my eye on college and a self-made life in this country. I hoped to become a psychologist with a focus on helping people from other cultures—people who aspired to be more but weren't familiar with America's customs and traditions. I had learned, by that point, that you can be defeated again and again, but that is okay if it motivates you to show your true beauty. Mispronouncing a word and then feeling the wrath of embarrassment from it taught me that when faced with adversity, I should ask myself, *What can I get out of this?*

Yes, I became bilingual, all right. I was the only Hispanic among five hundred and sixty six students who graduated with honors in the National Honor Society and the German Honor Society. Studying German allowed me to become even more articulate. People thought I was crazy to come to this country and learn a whole other language as a sophomore, but I loved it. I applied my proven process of learning a language to German, and it allowed me to be more proficient in English as well. Once I untangled German, it became easy to apply the same techniques that I had used to learn English.

In whatever language I chose, I vowed never to give up, which turned out to be a necessary promise. The fight of my life lay ahead, and I would need my mother's faith, my youthful stubbornness, and my persistent heart to overcome it.

## *Fig Factor: Persistence*

It isn't often that someone says failure is a good thing. But, guess what? It is. In fact, failure is a great thing if it motivates you to go one more round, to persevere beyond what you even thought possible. Persistence, then, is a life choice that will help you realize commitments and achieve incredible things. And the most important person to be accountable to is... you.

## Stepping stones to The Fig Factors . . .

1. When you close your eyes and envision your dreams, what do you see?
2. What mistake have you made in your life that proved to be a true learning lesson?
3. Where do you find your greatest motivation?
4. What is the hardest challenge you have faced, and what personal quality helped you overcome it?

# PART THREE:
*Some Buds Bloom,*
*Others Wither*

# 5

# THORNS AND ROSES

*"Ten percent is what happens,*
*and ninety percent is how you react."*

— Kevin Doyle

Our heart's deepest hopes outline our days. Like a grand orchestral movement falling and rising in rhythm and tonal character, hope changes as we change. We are swept along life in fast-running crescendos followed by heartbreaking minuets, soft and slow. And hope, a sister to our deepest dreams, re-imagines itself over and over again.

My hope throughout high school was to attend college. After a lifetime of reading, I knew education unlocked incredible opportunities, and I was fully prepared to embrace mine. Then, maybe when I was around twenty-six or twenty-seven, I thought I would plan my dream wedding and settle down.

Fate intervened.

Dad was preparing for a one-month trip to Mexico. For weeks, he packed unusual items for such a short trip: a bike, tools, pictures, clothes for all seasons. Meanwhile, our daily routine continued—Dad upholstered furniture, his hands rough from the pounding of nail heads, while my mom wrote poetry, cleaned the house, and made us meals that became quieter and quieter in the days leading up to Dad's trip. My own routine was edged in bewilderment.

"Why are you taking these things to Mexico?" we asked him. He told us they would fetch a good price there and he could always rebuy them here.

On the day of his departure, a yellow pick-up truck was nearly bursting with belongings I didn't even know we owned. Dad hugged and kissed me goodbye. *I'm coming back. I am.* But all those things he was taking with him... the long, hard hug he gave me, the cash he stuffed in my hand, and then his words, uttered in a deep voice, laced with sandy grit: "Take care of your mother, Jackie, and take care of yourself. You are a good girl, a smart girl." His eyes never met mine that day.

The truck's exhaust swirled into the sun-soaked air. A sense of loss engulfed me as my mom and I watched the yellow truck get smaller and smaller.

A month passed. Two months and then three. The endless ringing when we tried to call him became so expected that I think if someone had answered on his end, it would have startled us into hanging up. Finally, one day, he did answer. Mom's conversation with him only lasted a minute or two, and she wiped away tears from her pretty cheeks. The click of the phone entwined with her sobs. "He has asked us not to call him anymore," she said, her voice stunned as she stared the phone. "Your dad is not coming back."

Your dad is not coming back. YOUR DAD IS NOT COMING BACK. The words echoed in my ears, and images of him leaving our home in Malpaso flooded my mind: the back of his black t-shirt and blue jeans walking away, a bottle in his hand, a slam of the car door, the revving of the engine, the car getting smaller. I had seen it a hundred times, but a panic surged through me as I realized I had witnessed his last walk . . . away from me. Added to that was the realization that he had planned this departure for a long time. My heart ached at the thought of each time I looked at him and he knew. When we had breakfast on Sunday mornings, didn't you wonder what life would be like without me at the kitchen table? *When I came home from school and shared my day with you, didn't you think about the days ahead when you wouldn't hear my voice?*

Even the most resilient of us, at times, find ourselves broken. I was a heap of feelings and heart, and the tears I wanted to shed the day he left gave way. The dim light of the kitchen glowed coldly as my mom sat at the table. Breathlessly, I hugged her tightly. "I don't know how, but everything will be all right," I told her, crying. "Don't worry—I will take care of you," I lied without hesitating. I did the math and knew we didn't have the money to go on much longer. My consolations were broad statements of bravado, but I didn't care. I would figure it out.

Night's darkness crept inside, and the day's end symbolized the closing of a long, rocky road with my father.

* * *

As days and then weeks passed, the worst of the aftermath wasn't the lack of money or even Dad's absence. It was the rough, heavy guilt I heaped upon my shoulders. What had I done wrong? What could I have done to avoid this? What if I had not told him I wanted to come here? What if we had stayed in Mexico?

Yes, he had stopped drinking when he came to the United States. My mother never felt the hot strike of his hand as she sometimes had in Mexico. We were together—finally, together— as a family here in this country. But when Mom shared Dad's words that day, I realized that he had never embraced his new life. I had heard their arguments concerning money and the lack of time they spent together. I had watched Dad's unhappiness grow over the years. I had felt the wetness of my mother's tears as I wiped them away, but I never imagined he would truly leave. I always fiercely believed in the loyalty of love: love bends to sacrifice. Love endures. Love triumphs over weaknesses, mistakes, and selfish yearnings. Love keeps us grounded. So why weren't we enough of a reason to stay?

When I look back, I don't think Dad ever left Mexico in the first place. He would say, "See, you are spending ten dollars for this, which is one hundred and twenty pesos. Be careful how you spend your money—it could be a lot more if you were living in Mexico." Every reference was to Mexico, Mexico, Mexico. My mom pleaded, "But we are not in Mexico, we are here. Live in the moment, Jesus."

But he couldn't.

In a perfect world, a family would be the sustenance a father needs. I knew he carried an extra burden—the lack of his own father's support—all his life, but that didn't ease my own pain when I realized he knew, as he planned for his trip, that he'd never return. Had I seen hesitation in his eyes, an outline of regret, the day he left? I searched for it in my memory. I hoped for it.

In the end, I accepted Dad's departure as a challenge but not with the brightness and innocence I had in triumphing over my schoolwork. I rallied at the loss but with a strand of defeat for the first time in my life. I was my father's daughter in that he always pursued success, but I had learned a hard lesson from him: commitment to success or to a dream must work around the people you love—not the other way around. My dad and I differed on this point. I filed this knowledge away and vowed to break the cycle when I someday had children. They would have a mother and a father to watch over them. Of that, I was certain.

In the meantime, my plans for college—along with the rest of our lives—were derailed. Not being bilingual made it difficult for my mom to find a good job. My brothers were married and lived an hour away with their own families. I now needed to become the sole provider of our home. My pink world was over, and I realized that we would not be able to survive or would need to depend on my brothers, which seemed an impossible thing to ask of them at that time. So I took on a full-time job with a major hotel chain.

My mom stood steadfast in her faith. She was so sad, though, all the time. Of course, she and my dad had fought, but she never expected their marriage—a covenant of the most sacred kind in God's eyes and hers—to end in such a cold, abrupt way. Rings under her eyes marked the nights she pondered the days leading up to Dad's departure. She wondered why she hadn't seen the clues or read his mind. Most devastating to her, though, was that she knew my dreams of an education were on hold. To her, the pain of my sacrifice came second only to the word my dad used that day when she called and he finally answered.

He asked that we not "bother" him anymore.

\* \* \*

On the heels of one man leaving my life, another unexpectedly appeared. Juan Pablo Ruiz was a friend of my brothers and cousins, an extra at parties—a boy who loved music, soccer, and drawing funny pictures. His smile was sweet, his shyness endearing. We had been acquaintances throughout my adolescent years. Then, at the urging of my cousin, Juan Pablo asked me on a date.

The thumping, rhythmic beat of Cher's "Believe" blasted from my boom box as I dressed for the evening. White leather jacket with fox trim around the collar and cuffs: check. Jeans and boots: check. Hair slightly messy in a magazine page way: check. My mom smiled. She liked to see me happy, and I loved getting dressed up. Tonight, though, felt different. After years of playing cards, hanging out, and lobbing volleyballs to each other (I nearly took his head off a couple of times with a mean spike), Juan Pablo and I were about to play grownups and step outside from the diversions we had hidden behind for years.

We sat at a tiny table with white cloth napkins at Mario's Restaurant. A small candle between us illuminated his dark eyes. It hadn't been easy for him to get a night off from the private country club where he worked, but after two weeks of cajoling, he'd finally found someone to cover his shift. Christmas music played overhead as we smiled in disbelief: after years of quiet admiration, we were here. Still, I wasn't sure—was this a date or just a friendly outing? I didn't want to make any assumptions.

Then we started talking, and he began where all good things begin—with honesty.

"I remember the first time I saw you. It was at a restaurant," he ventured, smiling. "I remember every time after, too . . . until, finally, I had the courage to ask your cousin Fernando about you."

"Oh, really?" I flirted back, laughing. "What did you ask?"

He looked at me with sudden seriousness, his brow slighted furrowed, his jaw set. "I asked him for his blessing. I asked him if he thought I had a chance." He looked away for a moment, as though reminding himself he was now far beyond the point of pulling back. Juan Pablo's hands spread flat on the small table and he leaned slightly forward. "He encouraged me. He told me who you were dating and what a joke he was. He liked that I came from a good family and said that I should get to know you because . . ." he hesitated and let the last words out like a child releasing air after holding his breath for a long time, "we would be good for each other."

I sat back as my heart washed upon a new and vivid shore. Suddenly, I felt not so alone. I felt, a bit free, light, grateful. Could this be the man with whom I would spend the rest of my life? I never thought I would feel this way at this age, but it was swift and real—an epiphany of the heart. All the small things he had done over the years flashed before me—pulling out a chair or opening a door or asking how I was doing on a typical day. We had navigated through a magnetic field for years with stolen looks and nervous banter. Now, I felt like a long-time lottery winner with the prize only just revealed. I was falling in love.

A flood of conversation ensued. We tripped over our words, and when we thought there couldn't possibly be anything left to talk about, a freight train of new topics sped forth. We discovered that we came to the United States the same year, from the same area of Mexico. The priest from his church was the visiting priest in mine. Juan Pablo was born in Teocaltiche, Jalisco, a city just forty minutes from my small town of Malpaso. Had we remained in Mexico, however, we would never have met. There would have been no reason to skirt the mountain that separated our towns. Our paths would never have crossed.

Two weeks later, Juan Pablo asked me a question that I realized later was a litmus test for our relationship.

"What shall I tell your cousin we are?" he asked.

"Tell them I'm your girlfriend," I replied. For the first time ever, Juan Pablo Ruiz took a girl home to meet his family. I saw generosity in their welcoming hugs, respect in the way they spoke to one another, and a family rooted in loyalty as they helped and cared for each other.

Juan Pablo's first Christmas present to me symbolizes why he captured my heart. It wasn't about the present but the spirit with which it was given: he gave me a laptop because he thought it would help me with my college classes. He even took it to Macy's and had them wrap it in crisp, cream and gold patterned paper with a beautiful gold ribbon. Since then, Juan Pablo has fulfilled every dream I have ever had as a husband, a friend, and a business partner. From cooked lobsters, to a limo into the city to eat our favorite carrot cake, we celebrated the anniversary of our first date each following month. Then, one night, he took me out to dinner to a Brazilian restaurant and held my hands in his. From across the table, he looked deeply into my eyes.

"I don't want you to be only my girlfriend anymore," he said softly, almost in a whisper, "because I want you to be my wife."

In a thick voice, I cried, "Yes, yes, yes." I didn't see the people in the restaurant or the food on my plate or the early morning I had the next day. I saw my future, and it told of a beautiful journey that I would share with a man I truly loved. The ring he slipped onto my finger was a symbol of family and faith and forever.

Ten months later, I walked down the aisle wearing a white satin dress, my now-brown hair swept up with a pearl comb my mother had given me. Juan Pablo and I exchanged our vows in a small Catholic church a few towns over from the home my mom and I shared in Elmhurst. My mom's beautiful voice solemnly sang Ave Maria in Latin a cappella. Our eyes met, and I knew she was singing a true prayer that I would have the Blessed Mother's grace throughout my marriage. Her singing was the best gift she could have given Juan Pablo and me. A new life had begun.

A funny thing about the path we all walk is that just when a person thinks she has everything to be grateful for, she discovers the capacity for more.

Often, such wisdom is tied to heartache.

Juan Pablo and I had spent an afternoon with my brothers in Hoffman Estates. Now that we all had spouses, it made meeting up even more fun. I loved how Efrain peppered me with questions about my four-month-old marriage, always making sure I was happy, just as he had years ago. I sat in the passenger seat with the orange-violet sun washing over me through the glass, that feeling of contented fullness almost lulling me to sleep amidst a random stream of conversation about our future. I was twenty-one and Juan Pablo twenty-three. Madly in love, we reveled in dreaming about where we might eventually settle, what our career paths would be, and when we would have children. Amidst our conversation, my mobile phone rang.

"That's weird," I said, looking at the caller ID.

Juan Pablo looked at me quizzically. "Who is it?"

"My doctor." I had gone in for a routine medical exam a week earlier. Her call on a Thursday evening surprised me, and I felt a flutter of nerves as I answered the call. It was for good reason.

"Jackie," my doctor said, "I need you to listen. After looking over the results of your tests, we've found something. There's no way around what I am about to say. You have cancer. And you will need surgery immediately. Stop by the office tomorrow..." Her words faded into the night.

Cancer.

The tall office buildings, the passing cars, and the sumptuous sky all blurred as I took in her words. All I saw was the word "cancer" in big, black letters, forever changing my future.

I had heard the word on the news and read it in magazines. People I knew talked about it, but I had never associated it with my body. Diagnostically, said my doctor, it was cervical pre-cancer level four.

"Do people die of this?" I asked.

My doctor sighed. "I don't want to scare you. I know this is a lot for you to take in. I just can't underscore enough how surgery is something we need to do right away. That's what I am trying to get across."

But I didn't want to hear that. I wanted to hear that this wasn't serious and that everything was going to be okay, so I bit into my question like a pit bull, not willing to sacrifice anything short of the truth. I care what my doctor who didn't have cancer intended to achieve in this phone call. I needed to know what it meant for *me*.

"I am asking you if people die from this," I repeated, my voice far stronger than I felt. Beside me, Juan Pablo's face had gone pale.

Tentatively, my doctor told me of a case where a patient, also from Mexico, went back to her homeland to be with her family, ignoring treatment. The girl, just twenty-five years old, survived for three years before the cancer won. By now, we were almost home.

"Thank you," I said, unsure why I was thanking someone who just delivered such bad news. But I knew my doctor was just the messenger and a concerned one as well. I threw the phone into my purse and stared at Juan Pablo, searching for a way to explain what seemed unexplainable to me. Arrows of reality cut into a casual drive home after a beautiful day with family.

Outside our apartment, the man I loved put the car in park. The moment stood still. Somewhere in the distance, people were laughing and a car door slammed. It was the everyday noise of life. I took Juan Pablo's hand, and I told him what the doctor had said about the imminent surgery and the girl in Mexico. He kept his gaze on our hands, entwined between us, and then looked up at me with his lips set tight, defiance in his eyes. "Let's go in," he said. We walked up the stairs to our apartment and fell on the couch, two souls engulfed in silence.

\* \* \*

Fear leads our minds to dark places, and for days after the call, I saw my life in terms of goodbyes and last times. I mourned for the things I had not yet done, the children I had not yet conceived. I wanted to wake up from a horrible dream where hope had given way to uncertainty and despair. And while I trudged through the emotional devastation, what I felt most was guilt. Again, the image of my dad leaving us surfaced, and somehow I juxtaposed it with the news of my illness—only this time, I was the one who might be leaving. I was devastated that my new, loving husband had to experience this journey with me so early in our marriage. The burden was hard to swallow. I envisioned death and thought about what it would mean to my family if I weren't there. I thought about the dreams that would be left behind because I wouldn't be alive to accomplish them. I was just starting my life amid an incredible amount of joy and happiness as a married woman, so ... why now?

With Juan Pablo's love and my mother's prayers, I slowly understood what was before me. My first step was recognizing, with awe, my own vulnerability. Then I replaced the hurt and guilt with acceptance and objectivism. *If I have to do this, then I should prepare for it.* After feeling every kind of emotion, I was finally ready to fight it head on—whatever that meant. Once I accepted the situation, I was ready to embrace doing something to change it.

The date was set. I was mentally preparing by learning all I could about the surgery, adjusting my work schedule, and taking care of my physical wellbeing when suddenly I felt a terrible pain. The doctor said it had nothing to do with the cancer—cancer itself doesn't hurt, she told me. She was right; the pain wasn't from the cancer but from a cyst in the sub-urethral area near the cervix. Again, they said I had to have surgery and, no, the two could not be done at the same time—two surgeries in two weeks!

I was scared; who wouldn't be? I had never experienced any major medical procedure. The hospital staff, though, was professional and seemed to care genuinely about me. Conversation centered around their families; I tried to spark discussions that would make them happy or laugh just to push down my own fears for both my sake and Juan Pablo's.

"Do you like being a nurse?" I asked Joan, the nurse with a short brown bob. "Love it," she said as she took my pulse. "Nice break from my four kids. My husband appreciates me a whole lot more since I've gone back to work, too."

I laughed, finding it  at this because I thought how interesting that people need to be away sometimes to be understood. I did not know how this amazing medical team would handle the procedure, but I became open to whatever they had to do. Joan started the IV in as good-natured a way as  a manicurist takes the hand of a regular client, friendly and without fuss.

As they began wheeling me to the operating room, my hands were at my sides, clutching and then releasing the soft white sheet; the cotton was something tangible to hang onto. I said goodbye to Juan Pablo with tears in my eyes. Then, after a minute or two, I was out.

I woke up in a room feeling safe at the sight of a familiar face framed by the ceiling light: one of the nurses who had helped prep me before surgery looked almost like an angel. Her soft hands touched my arm lightly as she asked me if I knew where I was. I smiled and said, "Yes, the surgery is over." She seemed pleased that the anesthetic hadn't played with my memory. Juan Pablo walked in and took my other hand. For a moment, I felt reassured again that everything was going to be okay. And then I remembered the next surgery in just two weeks. It was a bittersweet moment.

When I returned for the second surgery, I expected the same professionalism, the same charismatic and caring staff, but it was different. The new team of nurses and staff were not as attentive as those on the previous visit had been, and I felt like a number rather than a patient. They took longer to care for me than the first time, doing their job in a detached, almost mechanical way. Of course, my only hope was that they would do a good job during my surgery. And they did. Relief washed over me as the second surgery ended. Never again would I take for granted a normal, ho-hum day. I craved being home and back into a regular routine.

My mother and brothers supported me, helping me heal with their love, their familiar touch. My mother visited often, Efrain brought us dinners weekly, and Salvador dotted my days with calls filled with teasing and humor. I knew he was trying to make me smile. Juan Pablo gave me soup when I was feeling weak. He took me to doctors' visits, hiding his worry for my health behind a mask of strength that I leaned on constantly.

The scars left by both surgeries ran much deeper than any wound to the flesh. In a final conversation before leaving the hospital, my doctor said, "Jackie, there is a chance you may never have children because of where the cancer started. You will most definitely be high risk. I think you and Juan Pablo should consider carefully the risks before you make a decision about having a family."

The words pinned photographs in my mind of my mother's miscarriages. I thought of my mom quietly praying in church before I was born and realized how much I wanted to be a mother. But it wasn't just about my life. It was about Juan Pablo's, too. He deserved to be a father as much as I desired to be a mother. I was only twenty-one years old—how could I simply accept what the doctor said? Though my own memories of my recovery are murky, my mom remembers that I was positive, and I did not take accept the prognosis. The inability to have children was simply not an option.

* * *

As an adult looking back on my life, I am grateful—not for my father leaving us but for the resolve, strength, and love I needed to meet it head on. I am grateful—not that my mother and I lost the stability and comfort of family life but for the opportunity to help her and test my own mettle along the way.

I am grateful—not for having cancer but for learning about my own vulnerability and the immense gift of being alive. I AM ALIVE. I wake up and open my eyes to the fragile nature of our existence. I AM ALIVE. I celebrate the chance to wrap my arms around my children, to help others in business, to smile and give people hope. I AM ALIVE. Our lives are gifts from God. I am, indeed, alive. And that alone is cause for celebration each day.

## *Fig Factor: Vulnerability*

When I became ill, I sought to strengthen my body by running. I adopted a vigilant workout schedule to build my immune system. I wanted my body to be strong and fit to fight whatever viruses I needed to combat. Coming face to face with a life-threatening illness redoubled my determination to triumph over it. Fortunately, running was an amazing discovery for me. The wind wraps around my body until I feel the presence of God. The challenge of going against what my body is telling me and instead relying on my mind and heart to move me forward is exhilarating. People yelling at the finish line, my breath barely keeping up with the beat of my heart, every fiber of my being pulsing with energy and fatigue... I crave those moments. The act of running is a great symbol for the value of vulnerability: we test ourselves against our own expectations not knowing beforehand whether we will lead or falter. In our everyday life, we open ourselves up to risk in exchange for self-growth, too. Author Brené Brown defines vulnerability as being "the core, the heart, the center, of meaningful experiences" in her book *Daring Greatly: How the Courage to Be Vulnerable Transforms the Way We Live, Love, Parent, and Lead*. Being open to the uncertainties of love, forgiveness, understanding, and even pain leads to a fuller life, a memorable life, a life truly lived.

## Stepping stones to The Fig Factors . . .

1. Can you recall a time when you felt extremely vulnerable? What did you learn?

2. If you were diagnosed with a serious illness, what would you be most grateful for?

3. How have you triumphed over extreme disappointment?

4. Where do you find inner strength?

5. What quote comes to mind that reminds you of your vulnerability?

## 6

# FIRST BLOOMS OF ENTREPRENEURSHIP

*"All the answers are inside of you."*

— Rhonda Byrne

Not many people use pizza as a pregnancy test. However, as we visited a friend's house two months after my surgery, this crowning king of American food nourished a part of me deep inside before I even took a bite. I love Hawaiian pizza. The juicy pineapple mixed with the salt of ham is outrageously delicious. But when the pizza arrived, I was repulsed by it.

"I bet you're pregnant!" shouted Juan Pablos's friend. My husband and I exchanged dumbfounded glances. It couldn't be. We weren't even trying! And besides, only sixty days earlier, my doctor had tried convincing me that pregnancy was outside the realm of what I could expect from my life. But then again . . . I stared at my pizza. The smell of warm cheese and tangy pineapple rose to meet me, nearly making me gag.

Juan Pablo and I raced to our local grocery store, bought a

test, and rushed home to take it. Impossible. We returned to the store and bought four more. The next day, I called my doctor and said, "There's no way. But I took five tests and they all show it as a plus."

After a long pause, he said, "Jackie, congratulations. You are going to be a mother. But listen carefully—the pregnancy will not be easy. You will need to come see me every week, and we will be watching you to make sure the baby is growing and developing." I nodded, too overwhelmed with joy and disbelief to let the doctor's words pierce me.

As time progressed, Juan Pablo and I felt as though we were visiting the baby on a weekly basis rather than visiting the doctor. There he was, this beautiful shape growing in my belly. Day by day, he changed from a tiny bean-like shadow to an unmistakable child. A boy. Visually inspired, Juan Pablo marked down the days to our baby's due date. One night, while in each other's arms, Juan Pablo said with a smile, "Can you imagine our baby when he is actually with us? How will he look? Will he have your beautiful eyes or my slender fingers?" And with a playful sidelong glance, he continued. "Will he be short like you or handsome like me?"

I responded, jabbing him in the side, "Probably he will take after me. My family has stronger genes, I think."

He said, "No way, the baby will look like me. I know that for sure. He will be tall and strong."

Giving in happily, I answered, "As long as the baby is healthy, I don't care how he looks."

Leonardo Ruiz screamed his way into the world during the early dawn of June 29, 2006. It was a gorgeous summer day, and I laid there completely spent. Juan Pablo gently lifted my hand to his lips and brushed it with an angel kiss. We giggled and cried, completely taken aback at the seven-pound, eleven-ounce miracle the nurse placed in my arms. A shock of black hair topped a beautiful baby boy who, the minute he heard his daddy's voice, opened his eyes wide in wonder. It was sweet love at first sight, a moment forever imprinted upon my heart. We had a son.

A handful of days later, I realized our small apartment had become the home I always dreamed of as a child. Mother, father, baby, love. The impact of Leo's life entwined with ours rushed over me all at once: he brought an abundance of joy and happiness—and responsibility. For the next twenty-four hours, three hundred and sixty five days, a decade, fifty years, a hundred years . . . he would be in our care., The elusive figure of Forever smiled at me and took my hand.

My life was transforming before my eyes. The tenor of my days had changed from meetings to feedings, from answering phone calls to answering my child's cries, from thinking only of myself and Juan Pablo to relishing every moment with our newborn son.

Before having Leo, I worked as a marketing director for Marriott Corporation, followed by a chain of Brazilian restaurants. My mother's faith outlined my foundation: I believed that I could do anything, and this naiveté gave me the freedom to dare and to learn, to make mistakes and try again as I refined my business skills. I discovered a passion for public relations, marketing strategy, and the challenge to make things happen as I oversaw a half-million dollar advertising budget for the restaurant chain with locations in downtown Chicago, Downers Grove, and Schaumburg. During my three-year tenure there, a world of opportunity grew. In tandem with earning my marketing degree at College of DuPage, I was spearheading events that connected me to a parade of high profile celebrities like David Beckham and his entire Real Madrid soccer team, executives from the Museum of Contemporary Art, CEOs from companies like Boeing and AM Corporation, and many editorial and advertising media contacts. The thrill of making people's dreams come true through marketing ignited a spark inside me that has never dimmed.

Once, a hotel manager who was a self-admitted marketing skeptic approached me with happy disbelief on his face. "Jackie, at first, I had no idea what marketing was and did not even believe in it," he said, "but your ideas are working. Last night we had forty new people for dinner who came in with a certificate from your hotel promotion. That is incredible—keep up the great work!" Inside, the little girl with high marks on her report card beamed.

Each time I received a complimentary remark about my work or an offer of a job, I took it with great joy. I realized that my make-it-happen attitude and my eagerness to get results and bring value, when combined with my positivity, attracted people to me. These traits had always been a part of me, but I had never realized they were different or special. Now, my resolve—to earn high marks in school, to conquer the English language, to push myself to run farther and faster—was applied to business. And I loved the challenge!

Early on in my career, sales were a large component of my job. It required a certain amount of pushiness, because if you did not have a signed document, you did not have a sale. Through marketing, however, I could inspire people rather than tell them what and when to buy. Marketing was a beautiful new world, and I loved it. *I can use my talent to create new ideas, help others implement them, and see the results,* I thought excitedly. And my ideas were working: people were coming into the restaurant through the promotions I created, and that fueled my passion. I started imagining what I could do for other businesses if they gave me the chance to help them. I wanted to experience their success and growth. Through marketing, I could make a true impact in the world; that was why I became so passionate about it—and I still am. I will do this for the rest of my life.

While working with the Brazilian restaurants, I gained the experience of being an "intrapreneur"—an entrepreneur within a company. The ability to connect with people, create marketing campaigns, see the results, and develop new ideas fascinated me.

I saw the industry greats, such as public relations maven Margie Korshak—a woman with a story much like mine—and dreamed that one day I would have a company like hers, complete with staff, special events, industry awards, and satisfied clients.

The time set aside for my maternity leave went by quickly. I pushed down the panic of returning to twelve-hour days, daily travel in and out of Chicago, and a job that, while exciting, suddenly seemed limiting with its moderate salary and expected annual raises. I had a son now and envisioned a future with no boundaries for him, for our family, and for me. A fierce desire to make something new, something different than I had ever known, crept its way to the forefront of my mind. The time to leap, to start my own business, was now.

The pages of my youth flipped before me as I continued my daily routine of changing diapers and watching Leo's tiny chest rise and fall in deep slumber. *All the answers are inside of you,* whispered Rhonda Byrne. *Whatever your mind can conceive, you can achieve,* said Napoleon Hill. *Everything you ever wanted is on the other side of fear,* shared Clark Weber.

I grabbed their wisdom, my thoughts urging me forward. I reassessed my life and realized that, of all the people I had ever known, one person had now inspired me to alter my course: Leo. One evening, I held him in my arms and looked into his sleepy eyes in earnest, the scent of his delicate skin rushing my senses and deepening my devotion to his little life. Scenes from my own childhood flashed before me: the people of Malpaso and their staunch opinions of my family, the loss of our home from the fire, my mom's hard work to earn a living for our family, the loneliness I felt when my brothers left, and the absence of my dad when I needed him most. I reflected on many instances where people were rooted in one spot.

"Leo, I promise you," I whispered, "I will not do that to you. Your dad and I are going to make a life for you in which you can do anything, be anything. We will always take care of you. I will always be with you. And I will always, always love you."

Leo's birth rearranged and then architected my life's vision. I suddenly felt . . . awake. I wanted a business with every fiber of my being. It was as though Leo's entrance into the world gave me permission to be the person I had waited all my life to become: an entrepreneur successful in making a mark in the lives of others. One thing I learned from reading great literature is that all the success you will ever achieve is in direct proportion to how many people you help become successful. When I was young, I did not know how to do this. Do you give people flowers to celebrate their successes? Write them notes of encouragement or offer your advice? Suddenly, as an adult, I knew. It was right in front of me: If I helped others grow their businesses, they would enjoy success not only professionally but personally, too. It would allow them to achieve their dreams, have financial independence, and provide for their families. The impact of marketing was all encompassing and awe inspiring.

Books, again, were strewn across my bed, the couch, and my kitchen counter. Juan Pablo questioned my Amazon orders and the sheer volume of book-sized boxes coming to the house. As I fed Leo, I flipped pages on how to start a corporation in Illinois. I struggled to keep my eyes open to finish a chapter on pricing services and the principles of great client service. I considered a name and corporate colors; a colleague suggested blue or purple because they were subtle colors that were appealing to the eye. While folding laundry one day, I chose a rich, eggplant purple because it was vibrant and hopeful. I sought to learn everything it would take to open up JJR Marketing Consultants—as I decided to call my company—only to find out later how much there was left to discover.

When Leo was four months old, I packaged him up in his baby carrier and went to visit a SCORE consultant at Harper College. Staffed by retired business executives, SCORE is a free resource available to entrepreneurs in many cities nationwide. I checked in with a receptionist who was pleasant, waited a couple of minutes, and followed her into a resource room lit by bright fluorescent overhead lighting and decorated sparingly with furniture placed around the room. An older gentleman in his late sixties with white hair and a beautiful smile greeted me. There were several books lying on the desk, and I was tempted to glance at their titles but chose to focus on the important conversation instead.

"What are your dreams?" the SCORE advisor asked.

I shared my idea of starting a marketing agency, and he seemed more interested as the minutes flew by. He "saw" my passion, he said. He got it. Then he asked me, "What do you think marketing is?" Instantly, I flashed back to my dad asking if I wanted to go to the United States. *More than anything, Dad, I want to go.* Again, I was being asked to reach inside myself and face a truth. Somehow, I knew this moment would define which direction my life would take.

With all the passion, all the fierce belief that starting a business was the right thing to do, I said, "Marketing is what makes good companies great. I want to help as many businesses as possible be leaders, be known, connect with their customers, and grow."

In a single sentence, my hopes and dreams became real. He smiled brilliantly. "Jackie," he said, "you are ready."

I had hoped to get one thing out of this meeting: validation. I believed that this was the right time to start my business, that it was meant to be, but I needed someone to verify this, and he did. This was the single most important bridge that led me to launch my business with confidence. I walked out of there ready to make a difference in the world as an entrepreneur!

Others in my life, however, were mystified. My mother-in-law, my friends—even Juan Pablo—questioned my decision. Their definition of "who" I should be differed from mine. A stay-at-home mom? An employee with the security of benefits and a paycheck? A part-time staffer doing repetitive work? It is easy to look back and understand their skepticism. I was twenty-three years old, had never owned a business, had just delivered my first baby, and was about to graduate from college. Who was I to start my own business? Fair enough, but . . . who was I not to start it? My mother-in-law, one of the sweetest, most loving people I know, took me to task the strongest. We were visiting her and, with a lot of enthusiasm, I shared with her my dreams of starting a business. Her brow furrowed as she busied her hands at the stove, pushing garlic around in a pan with a wooden spoon.

"What do you think you are doing?" she asked. "You have a new baby, and your only concern right now should be taking care of him."

My spirit crashed. "I want to give Leo a better life. If this takes off, Juan Pablo won't have to work those long, crazy hours." I fought for my ideas in the name of her son. Proud, stubborn, and hurt, I licked my wounds and sat mostly silent the rest of the evening.

As a mother of two now, I realize her concern for our family inspired her wariness. Besides, entrepreneurism is a difficult concept for many people to understand. Juan Pablo was a bartender at a private country club, and no one in his immediate family had a business, so he did not have an example with which to compare my entrepreneurial dreams. It seemed to him and others that all odds were against me. I was young, Hispanic, female, a new mom. He questioned where I was going when I left the house, what clothes I wore, who I was meeting, and when I would be back. Later, when he joined me as a partner, he understood much better the demands on my time, but it was hard for him to see them clearly early on. He was, at that point, outside my career world looking in.

A barrage of negativity, an empty canvas, a stack of books, a determined heart, and a vision sketched out this new adventure. The light that sparked my business was impossible to ignore. I had found my career vocation, my calling, and I knew it.

As I recall the time in my life when I first launched my business, I am grateful. A son was born. A company was born. And I learned that following one's heart rarely takes you down the wrong path . . . because the pain of regret is far greater than the pain of failure.

Despite what people said and thought, I knew in my heart that starting a business was the right thing to do. I envisioned myself ten years later as a successful entrepreneur with staff and accolades, a beautiful purple office, and a great reputation. Where did this vision take me? I am sitting here now, surrounded by my eggplant-colored walls lined with nearly twenty industry plaques and trophies, a talented team of people working for us, and a stable of clients who, on any given day, send me a note of thanks. Here's what I know for sure: if I can see it, I can do it.

Later, I would again be forced to take these words to heart.

# *Fig Factor: Vision*

Contemplate the layers of a brick structure and imagine what would happen if even one layer was weak or missing. We have layers, too, that reveal our authentic selves and help shape the vision for what we can become in the future. Regarding them gives us clarity and direction. So does drawing on strength from others. Having just one person validate my vision fed my courage to launch a business. Believing in others and drawing strength from them will help you realize your vision, too.

**Stepping stones to The Fig Factors . . .**

1. Close your eyes and envision yourself five years from now. Draw a circle with your vision in the middle. Then outline the steps you need to take to ensure you arrive at your desired destination.

2. Who are the top advocates in your life? How do they support you? When was the last time you told them how much they mean to you?

3. What qualities do you possess that have prepared you to fulfill your vision?

# 7

# FLOWERS IN FALL

*"Onement, is being present in one single moment of time."*

— Jennifer Weggeman

In December 2006, baby Leo and JJR Marketing shared a birthday of five months. In those early days, I woke up every morning and got ready for work, choosing either my black suit jacket and pants or purple jacket and black pants. My make-up routine was simple: cream foundation, two-toned brown eye shadow to match my eyes, black eyeliner, a swoosh of mascara, and a quick brush of blush. I hesitated as I looked in the mirror each morning, remembering my mother's words: dress for success. As I fulfilled a dream of starting my own business, I knew I was living out my mom's dream as well. *The flowers in fall are just as beautiful, Mom. Each stride I take counts for both of us.*

When I was ready, which was not much past eight each morning, I walked ten steps to the little room in our apartment set aside for my office. It didn't matter if I had a meeting or not, I was committed to always dressing for my job as an independent marketing executive. A desk, computer, bookshelf, and silver waste can awaited me. There wasn't room for much else. Sometimes Leo accompanied me, and I strategically timed phone calls during his naps. It became the how-to-talk-on-the-phone-when-Leo-wasn't-crying game. I mostly always won as Juan Pablo still worked nights at the country club and rushed in as a backup player for my side of the contest during the day.

On my desk, stacks of paper grew from my perpetual documentation: meeting reminders, letters, client brochures, notes from well-read books, business articles torn savagely from magazines, my dreams in flow chart form, heavy college tomes from my last semester, file folders for each subject, and endless lists. My theory is that when you don't quite know what you are doing, you feel compelled to save every shred of paper if for no other reason than to have proof of your workday. I had plenty of proof.

At that five-month mark, stores and houses were dressed for Christmas with breathy trees, sumptuous gold and silver ribbons, and sparkling lights. I loved the prospect of picking out the first round of oversized plastic toys that we would somehow figure out how to assemble for Leo, clothes for Juan Pablo, and a beautiful scarf and purse for Mom. I wanted only one thing: a new cell phone! The Blackberry was the smartphone of choice, and I wanted one. (Hard to believe now, but iPhones didn't even exist at the time.)

Juan Pablo and I didn't have a lot of money, but we were happy. Somehow, the pieces of my life were arranged in a way that, for the first time, made sense to me. Like a mosaic with hundreds of small tiles placed precisely into an image, my path as a mother, wife, and businesswoman was sure and confident. My clients, mostly restaurants early on, hired me to draft marketing plans, send press releases to the local media, and create promotions and special events. While Juan Pablo and the rest of my family were still skeptical, I knew that if I just worked hard enough, my business would be successful. I could see nothing standing in my way.

Or so I thought.

The greatest fears for any runner are dog attacks, out-of-control cars, and unforeseen accidents. Runners fear these things because they are unexpected. Is running through life any different? We plan, we set down our best intentions, we refuse to see what could go wrong, and we aren't prepared when it happens.

Sometimes, the unexpected even creeps forward innocently, as was the case with the invitation to the Indian restaurant. Nestled in the quaint town of Westmont in Chicago's western suburbs, the prospective client was looking for a marketing plan for his newly opened restaurant. Donning my black suit— conservative, business-like—I kissed my mom, who lived just a few blocks away and sometimes babysat, and I hugged my little Leo goodbye and left for my meeting.

Much in the same way I had prepared for the speech that changed my high school years from unbearable to unbelievable, I mentally went over my key advantages and hospitality experience on the car ride over. Dale Carnegie had taught me that a prospect can't say "no" if you give them every reason to say "yes."

Intricately carved wooden animals, important symbols of the Hindu religion, adorned the burnt orange walls. Ivory lampshades suspended from the ceiling featured ornate iron scrollwork, giving the impression of undulating waves for the eye to navigate. A poppy red textile drizzled with coppery strands of silk hung on the far wall near a welcoming fireplace. These were the rich, sumptuous colors and textures I walked into that day. I felt the vibrancy of the Indian culture, almost as warm and inviting as the owner himself. Short, dark, and bespectacled, around forty years old, he said, "We searched for you. Six months. Happy to meet you. Thank you for coming here at such a busy time."

It is hard to imagine not being able to locate someone, but it wasn't as easy to track people then as it is now, especially given that my website wasn't complete yet, I had switched phone numbers during that time, and the restaurant wasn't quite sure of my company name. There was no LinkedIn, and Facebook had just debuted outside college campuses. MySpace was hot with seventy-five million users, but I declined to participate; to me, it wasn't a business tool. So, after hearing good things about me, the people at the Indian restaurant finally got my number from a chance conversation with someone who knew me. On that day, I stood before them grateful for the possibility of working with them.

Growing up Hispanic, coming to this country as a young girl, and surrounding myself with mostly American friends, I had never tasted Indian food. I was curious about the delicious aromas, smells inspired by orange, chicken, and a compendium of spices. But I took my cue from the short, fit man with the sand-toned skin: he didn't offer me any food. As I was leaving the restaurant, though, my eye caught three bowls near the cash register. They were smooth and glossy in bright russet orange and muted red and green, and each was filled with what looked like seeds or grains.

"What are those?" I asked.

"Oh, those are spices we use to cleanse the palette after eating," he responded.

I love learning about different cultures. Embracing other people opens one up to infinite possibilities for learning, opportunity, and helping others. "May I try?" I asked.

"Of course," he responded with an appreciative smile. I envisioned bringing culinary writers to the restaurant and asking them in a suave and worldly voice, *Would you like to cleanse your palette?*

I lifted the small spoon, choosing cardamom. A rush of brownish black seeds fell into the palm of my left hand.

"Ah, you have chosen the queen of spices," the owner said knowingly. Feeling almost regal tossing it inside my mouth, I said my final goodbyes and walked out the door.

Within a minute, an excruciating pain blossomed in my lower stomach. The cars in the parking lot drowned in a vague blur, and I struggled to remember where I had left my car. Once I found it, I collapsed within the arms of the leather driver's seat, both dizzy and nauseated.

*Focus, you're not far from home.* Chills ran up my arms. *Green means go, stay in the right lane.* As a runner, I knew about the power of deep breathing to keep pain at bay, but the shock waves inside me were beyond anything I had ever experienced. *Leo is counting on you...*

By sheer will, I made it home. My mom, whom Juan Pablo had already relieved from babysitting, came over immediately, hearing in my voice that something was incredibly wrong. When she arrived, she found me writhing on the floor. Juan Pablo had no idea what to do. He thought the attack might be an allergic reaction. We called my doctor, and he said to wait a little while to see if the pain would go away.

But it didn't go away. It got worse.

An inner war raged with pain triumphing. Once again, my blood was laced with fear—fear that I didn't know the cause of my ailment, fear that somehow the cancer had returned with a vengeance, fear that I would be too ill to take care of Leo, and fear that I wouldn't survive this, whatever this was. My mom gave me a bolillo, a type of Mexican bread roll, and tea. Steeped in exhaustion, I fell into painful sleep.

In the darkest part of night, I awoke itching everywhere on my body—my scalp, arms, stomach, legs, feet ... every inch of me begged attention. My urine was black and my bowel movements white. Fear had succumbed to panic. Something was terribly wrong. Again, my mom, a forever hero in my eyes, came over to stay with Leo, and Juan Pablo rushed me to the emergency room at Good Samaritan Hospital, just three miles away.

The car ride is a blur to me, but Juan Pablo later told me "I held your hand as though I were clutching a long rope on the side of a mountain so high its top was in the clouds. My survival was yours. And I determined that I would use my own will to make you better, and I would fight for you. I never loved you so much as I did in that moment."

A three-day parade of ultrasounds and tests with mysterious acronyms like ERCPs, MRIs, and HIDA scans pinpointed one possible problem: gallbladder stones. The reality was, though, doctors could not determine a cause with certainty. Too many of my symptoms were outside the scope of that simple diagnosis.

I was transferred to Northwestern Hospital, known for its gastrointestinal medical department. Another week went by and the start of another when they discovered a cyst, sly in its positioning between the gallbladder and liver, hiding amidst the bile ducts. Extrahepatic Choledocal Cyst Type II. It was the second rarest out of five different types of cyst—one in one hundred fifty thousand people get it, and the vast majority of them live in Japan. I had no relation to the Japanese culture. I had never even tasted sushi. Nothing made sense.

A plan was set: surgeons would remove part of the small area between the bile ducts and replace the space in between with a plastic stent. They sent me home for nearly three weeks before the surgery.

For any of us, what happens in the span of twenty-one days buried within an average month in an average year? We fold laundry, sleep, write emails, meet someone new, kiss, run, wake up and wish there were more minutes in the morning, cook dinner, make love, smile unexpectedly, argue with a spouse, try to get off the phone with a friend who loves to talk, shop for groceries, read a book, make a bed, shuttle kids to sports practices, and study for a test. Sometimes, we cry or help a friend or write a note. One thing we don't often do is cherish.

So, for three weeks—twenty-one straight days—I cherished. I saw life in a completely different way. Food tasted better. My family's hugs felt magical. I became awake, alert. Everything was more vivid. Everyday things like my husband's laundry on the bedroom floor or an unreturned phone call or Leo's toys strewn about didn't bother me anymore. I greedily drank in moments with my son, who was so giving with his generous smiles and whose physical warmth told me I was most definitely home to him. Had I seen how beautifully slender his little fingers were before as they wrapped around mine? Juan Pablo and I faced each other with a heartbreaking silence sometimes. Tender touches, my face on his chest, we solemnly swore that there would be no one else for either for us, ever. They were silly promises made in a sea of tears I didn't even know I had left in me. But an undercurrent swelled equally deep, an undercurrent of positivity. I had waited all my life to find my muse. Like a soldier protecting his garrison, I pledged not to give up any of it.

Getting ready for the surgery was a journey unto itself—like a dream vacation of sorts. I walked on a balance beam separated by two worlds: Gratitude, a place with brilliant light illuminated by my many blessings, and Fear, wrought by dark shadows and despair.

When I visited Gratitude, I saw life through a new lens. Blessings like the food in my refrigerator or waking from a deep sleep were unveiled to me with the drama of a million-dollar sculpture. I marveled at these simple things that had been there all my life. How had I missed them? When I traveled the road and passed the entrance to Fear, I fumbled in the dark to pick up cards, each one naming the moments I might never see again. Leo growing up, said one. My husband's brave heart, printed on another. Holidays with my mom. Barbecues with my brothers' families. Stark blackness lined the roads of Fear, and inevitably, tears rained fiercely, turning dirt into thick mud.

I vividly recall two experiences from this time. One taught me the power of the mind; the other, the power of the heart.

The first experience was during my three-week sojourn before surgery, when I was scheduled to present speech number seven out of ten at Toastmasters of Oak Brook. The end goal was a Competent Communicator certificate. In the history of that regional office, no one had gotten so far so quickly. I approached the podium, butterflies flying wild inside me. I was ready to put into practice all that Toastmasters had taught me—maintaining eye contact, disregarding distractions, balancing tonal quality, timing dramatic phrases, and creating trust with the audience.

Speech number seven was different because it would address my rare condition. Part of me was excited about the fact that I would be eighty percent of the way to getting my certificate at the close of this speech, but another part of me stumbled at the thought that I was so closely connected to the topic.

As though choosing a pistol for a duel, I considered my options and chose objectivity as my weapon to fight the emotional war simmering just below the surface. I walked to the corner conference room inside McDonald's corporate offices in the posh city of Oak Brook. Windows outlined the room with tables pushed together to form a U-shape. I set up graphs and charts and mentally prepared to address the three dozen or so people due to attend the meeting that day. Then, when everyone arrived, I began.

"You may think I am speaking a foreign language when I say the following, but I am not. It is simply the name of a rare condition with no real known cause that most people have never heard of: Extrahepatic Choledocal Cyst Type II. They say you will probably be of Asian descent to have it. Let me be the first to tell you, they are wrong." The audience laughed at my quips as I went on to explain how the flow of bile from the liver becomes blocked and other details about the condition. I closed by encouraging people to find out more and to ask their doctors about it.

As I spoke, I played a mind game, convincing myself that the person with that condition was someone else instead of me. Do not get emotional, I instructed myself in the moments I felt my throat start to close with familiar disbelief: *How can this be happening to me?* Instead, I told myself, *You're a professional. Give them the best speech they've ever heard from you.* As such, I was engaging, made eye contact, and avoided "ahs" and "ums" per the Toastmaster manual. I completely detached myself from the major surgery scheduled in two weeks.

When the speech was over, I leafed through the surveys filled out by attendees after the one-hour speech; comments were congratulatory on every count. My gratitude gave way to tears, my objectivity wholly sacrificed. I couldn't hold it in any longer and surrendered to my deep emotions and fears. Friends hugged me and wished me good luck. Everyone should be so fortunate to surround themselves with such "family" during difficult times.

I learned that day how the power of the mind is the balancing foundation for keeping emotional experiences in check. It brings objectivity when needed. My experience taught me to be strong and to show up with my best attitude, not burdening people with unnecessary negativity.

The second important experience took place Christmas Day with my family. I wore a red necklace with matching earrings, and a brown and white shirt. I felt open and in tune with life that particular day. My surgery, scheduled for January 9, was fast approaching, and I wasted not a day or an opportunity to let everyone know how much I loved them. Each of them meant so much to me.

Efrain, along with his beautiful wife and daughter, hosted Christmas. My entire family was there: my mom, brothers, and two cousins. I felt the heaviness in the air fueled by fear of the unknown. One by one, they told me how much they loved me and cared about me. When it came time to open presents, we sat on the big leather sectional and shared our gratitude before opening each gift. Almost everyone shared a good intention for my upcoming surgery, trying to be strong for me, though their voices were cracking. I could see in my mother's eyes that fear was taking its toll on her. She pulled me in for a hug any chance she got, telling me how much she loved me and reassuring me that everything would be okay. Not many people have an opportunity to witness true unconditional love from so many people in one room, at one time. I felt it and hoped it would never go away. This is what heaven is like, I believe. In heaven, everyone loves and is happy, all at the same time, all in one big room. I picture platters of food, a lack of all judgment and condemnation, and love without reason or cause. Love for the sake of loving. Love because we can. Infinite power of the heart.

My twenty-one days mended wounds, too, that otherwise would have been left open and sore, perhaps forever. "We fought so much as little girls. Please forgive the days between now and then that we haven't spoken," I told my cousin Lorena. We had grown up together, and everyone always confused us as identical twins. As in so many childhood relationships, time and miles had created a chasm between us that we finally repaired. We had a long, deep conversation about the meaning of life and the importance of prayer, a conversation I cherished deeply. Still, I did not have any communication with my dad during this time. While I didn't dwell on it, always in the back of my mind sat the little girl waiting for her father to come home and see her latest math grade. Only this wasn't about a grade. This was far more serious, and it required all of my focus.

January 9 was a steely cold day, the kind that is both invigorating and cutting. Juan Pablo drove me to Northwestern Hospital for the fourth time in two years, but today was different. There was far more at stake. I could feel his concern, so we talked about our favorite topic: the future.

"You will be okay, honey. I love you so much," he repeated.

"Leo should play soccer someday—he crawls with such big, strong kicks," I said.

A little later, Juan Pablo talked about his visions for our first house. "It's going to have a small patio out back so we can grill hamburgers, and it will have lots of windows and a basement for all my tools." He squeezed my hand. My heart turned upside down the way it did the moment he asked for my hand in marriage. With some comic relief, he looked at me sideways, eyebrows raised, and said, "And a nice big closet so my clothes have a chance of seeing a hanger."

We had a lot to live for together.

As we were about to get out of the car, I grabbed his arm. "I love you so much. I am afraid, Juan Pablo, but I will be strong for you and Leo." He wasn't just my husband any longer; he was the father of my son, changing my perspective on everything.

Inside the hospital, we were escorted to a little room with an empty desk and dim lighting. The doctor, a fit man in his mid-forties, explained it would require a couple of hours and reiterated that he would only remove the bile duct connecting the gallbladder to the liver and replace it with a plastic stent. At one point, I met his blue eyes head on and thought I caught something, a look that came and passed quickly but was definitely there. It was a look of apprehension.

We walked down the hall to where I prepared for the

surgery. A breezy cotton gown, Juan Pablo solidly by my side, I smoothed my hair back and counted backwards under sedation, but, in my mind, I was only looking forward...

...and then I awoke on the twentieth floor of a brick building in a beautiful hotel-like hospital room. I awoke to the sound of a deep, thoughtful voice, a trace of astonishment edging his speech.

"Jackie, your positive attitude saved you," said the doctor.

I didn't know what he meant. Then I noticed a freeway of tubes coming and going from everywhere along my body: a catheter and feeding tubes and an intravenous drip. I had envisioned this moment of waking many times, but I wasn't tangled in plastic ribbons in any of my fantasies.

"When we opened you up," the doctor said, "and prepared for the surgery we thought we were going to do, we noticed that the cyst was pre-cancer level four. The truth is that you could have died from this without even knowing. You were born with it. There's no way that you could have ever found it—except, when you ate the cardamom, it caused the cyst to swell so that it obstructed the passage of bile. That brought on the onset of the pain and other complications." He put this in perspective for me by adding, "Just imagine if you were driving down a road at eighty miles an hour on a twenty-mile-an-hour road. Of course, a police officer would notice that, but what if the police officer gets distracted for a split second as he takes a phone call and, because of this distraction, doesn't stop you from the inevitable tragedy of a crash. That's what happened to you. That's how close you were to having cancer that could have taken your life in five days, five months, or five years. This would have taken your life because it would have propagated in your digestive system. We had to remove the gallbladder and bile ducts, as well as cut the intestine in half and reconnect it to the liver."

"Thank you," I uttered. I didn't know what else to say. Shortly after that, he left. Onto another patient, another surgery, calls on hold. The door closed quietly, and sweet solitude befell the room.

I was grateful to be alone, for the luxury of privacy to reflect on the doctor's words. I felt so blessed at that moment—more than any other moment in my life. I looked up at the white ceiling of that room and could feel in my heart this message: *You are here to serve others.* God's message was clear. My mission, defined.

\* \* \*

At the hand of someone much larger than me, every step in my life has been for a reason.

If I had still lived in Mexico, I may not have had the care in a hospital specializing in gastrointestinal issues.

If I didn't have my family here, I would have been alone.

If I hadn't started JJR, I would never have been in an Indian restaurant.

If I didn't have the inspiration to embrace other cultures, I wouldn't have had the moxie to try a raw Indian spice.

If I didn't have Leo, I may not have redoubled my resolve to overcome physical obstacles.

Every single event that took place—how it happened, when it happened, why it happened—culminated to create a miracle. Six months later, Salvador shared with me that the doctor had told him that he could not promise I would make it through surgery. When my brothers had arrived that day, they demanded to talk with the doctor with the vehemence of a father. I realized that my brothers had taken on this parental role without ever making it obvious. A surge of emotion ran through me as I discovered my brothers' unwavering, fatherly love for their baby sister. They had advocated on my behalf, bravely and solidly. We have traveled far from the innocent chasing and name-calling of years ago, haven't we, Salvador?

Not a day is lost to me now. I am blessed to be alive and to know in my heart that I am here to serve others through every avenue of my life: my business, friendships, books I write, and the empathetic natures of my children Leo and my beautiful daughter Giulianna, who was born two years after the surgery. (We discovered my pregnancy after another Hawaiian pizza incident and multiple pregnancy tests!)

Everything aligned itself for the good that new year of

2007. My life was forever changed. Awareness, for a second time, took my hand and gracefully guided me forward to a new place of understanding.

# *Fig Factor: Awareness*

The odds of finding myself in a place and time that helped me discover, identify, and cure a rare condition I didn't even know I was born with revealed to me the mystical nature of life. I believe God watched over me for many years before I tasted the cardamom. All roads led to that moment because, without it, I would never have known about my condition. And what if I hadn't had been born with such a condition? What if I had lived my life without succumbing to such total awareness?

Would I repeat the journey just to learn what I have learned? Yes. Easiest question I have ever answered.

### Stepping stones to the Fig Factors . . .

1. How clearly do you know yourself? Pick a day and focus on your choices, actions, and exchanges with others. (For example, when you speak to your son about his day at school, do you stop and listen, or do you keep washing the dishes?) Find awareness in little moments.

2. How can you shift your perspective to see the everyday moments as extraordinary? What impact could this have on your life?

3. How would you spend twenty-one days before a life-changing experience? Who would you reach out to and what would you say?

# PART FOUR:
## *Seeds in the Wind*

# 8

# AFTERWORD:
# THE BEAUTY OF RAIN

*"Gratitude is the air I hope my children breathe
as they journey the world."*

— Jackie Camacho-Ruiz

Rain pours. I watch the droplets race down the window and disappear almost as abruptly as they land. There is a rhythm to the rain, a soft, intentional brushing of a distant drum, a concerto rising and falling with nature's sighs. It soothes me.

The scene makes me consider one of my favorite symbols: water. Water calls forth the image of blessings washing over me. Our hands cannot hold water for hours on end; we are compelled to let it go. Blessings, too, cannot be held too closely for too long. They live in the heart, a place where things are shared naturally. When we risk giving a part of ourselves to others—whether it's a compliment to a stranger or sleep lost to help a friend through her troubles—new life takes root. We have made a positive change for someone else, like a seed that finds its home after traveling miles on the wind.

Many of my experiences are the same ones people face every day. Extracting the beauty out of difficult situations, though, altered the outcomes for me. With astonishing influence, we can rewrite our script by defining beauty within the landscape of our life. Dale Carnegie said, "Today is our most precious possession. It is our only sure possession." Why, then, let our only sure possession tarnish by not appreciating it wholly and thoughtfully?

A little girl picks figs. And she is changed. As a child, I did not fully recognize the shift inside, but I see now that I was empowered by realizing I make something from seemingly nothing—just everyday fruits that people pass by and dismiss as insignificant. In doing so, I could help my mom and dad by making extra money, evoke smiles in others, and feel accomplished. Living the fig factors all started on that day.

And where did it lead me?

My business partner is my soul mate, giving a strong foundation to both journeys. Juan Pablo has helped me fulfill every dream I have had. As he discovered his talent as a graphic artist, he incorporated it into a business that gave us a life. He gave me the freedom to be what I needed to be. The miracle of our love has matured and evolved, nurturing our family in ways I pined for as a little girl.

I am a successful entrepreneur, and our business grows about thirty percent each year..People consider me a thought leader on marketing and public relations; I've given hundreds of speeches to colleges, corporations, and business groups across the country. I am a regular print, radio, and television guest locally and nationally, and a two-time published author.

Of the dozen or so awards displayed in my office, I am most proud of the Entrepreneurial Excellence Award from a prominent Chicago-area newspaper; the Latina Entrepreneur of the Year award from Chicago Latina Network; and the Outstanding Contribution Award from the Sheilah A. Doyle Foundation, a non-profit organization that helps children who have lost a parent or sibling through violence. I am a member of three boards of directors. I graduated with honors from both high school and college. My running carves out another personal milestone for me. My most gratifying accomplishment, however, is my children. They are healthy, happy and ... go figure, they love to read and explore the world. I came to this country with my family yearning to live the American dream. I am living it.

At the beginning of this journey, I invited you to walk with me. More than anything else, I wanted to give you a gift by sharing my discovery of how to live an amazing life. When I was a little girl in Mexico, I was the absolute worst at keeping a secret. Sharing the fig factors with you reminds me of my love for those tell-all moments—I could not keep these gems to myself. I want your vision to be panoramic and your life to be a journey of joy. I hope that, in the wake of your steps, people stop and think that you are different—that you stand for something much greater than yourself. Because inside all of us is our destiny, ready to take root.

Just like seeds in the wind.

# *Fig Factor: Passion*

Destiny is a place ahead of us. It is the horizon that our eyes see just before sleep. But the present moment leads to destiny. The here and now are the bricks and mortar that build our future, and we build it every single day.

I want to share with you the things I often do that help me feel happiness and celebrate life's little moments.

**1)** I love using the word "amazing." It may, at first, seem exaggerated; look it up and you'll find astonishing, awe-inspiring, breathtaking. Every time I say the word, something emotionally shifts and activates the positive part in my brain. Even when I am having a bad day, I match the word with the emotion and I can't frown. It's a great barometer to get me back on track.

**2)** Several times a week, I "feel" happiness. It is, after all, not an imagined emotion. Happiness is real and touchable and intentional. I pause, take a deep breath, and imagine my body is filling up with all the good things in my life. The blessings flow through me like rushing blue water—fresh, clean, and vibrant. This simple act brings me to the core of who I am in the present moment. Breathing happiness allows me to be grateful both physically and emotionally.

**3)** Even if you don't consider yourself a writer, pick up a journal. I write in my gratitude journal at least twice weekly. Rhonda Byrne, author of The Secret, inspired me on this point. On the left side of each page, I list the things I am grateful for; on the right, I list the things I desire. The hitch: I write the right side the same way I write the left! So, if I am hoping for a new client to come on board, I write: *I am grateful for this new company that has now become a client.* Gratitude is an accelerator to reaching your dreams in abundance. The act of gratitude creates a sense of love around you that helps you achieve your dreams.

**4)** Ask my kids the word that best describes me, and they will say I am silly. I love being silly. I come home, put on Dora the Explorer music, and dance with Leo and Giulianna. I enjoy it like a child. I travel to another world far away from the stresses of the office and the decisions I face, giving me a sense of freedom and creative inspiration. Why does being an adult mean we can't have fun?

**5)** The medical community has yet to put happiness in a pill. Exercise or being active is the closest I've experienced to "instant happiness." Sometimes, I take my kids places where we jump, feeling the lightness of life with every bounce. And, of course, running and being out in nature are two of my passions. Whatever you choose to bring you instant happiness, do it with overflowing gratitude.

# EPILOGUE:
## *Living the Fig Factors*

I have been blessed to know many special people who live the fig factors. Some of them are friends, some are clients, and others are colleagues. No matter their background, they are everyday people like you and me who have done extraordinary things with their lives. Just as I saw the figs outside my bedroom window in new and different ways, these people saw life with fresh eyes and made something of it that changed their course ... and brought a world of amazing positivity to many other people.

Kevin Doyle, founder and director of the Sheilah A. Doyle Foundation, honors the fig factor of **persistence** in the face of great adversity. At the age of seventeen, Kevin lost his mom. Without hesitation, he chose to turn the pain from tragedy into good. Today, he transforms the lives of children whose parents, legal guardians, or siblings were victims of homicide. His foundation provides grief counseling through free camps, college scholarships, and assistance to other not-for-profit organizations. What do I admire most about Kevin? His amazing outlook on life and his choice to make a difference in the lives of others whose pain he feels every day.

Corey Kelly, founder and owner of TriBalance, honors the fig factors of **wisdom** and **awareness.** After triumphing over depression and addiction, Corey gained unique insights into the obstacles faced by teenagers and adults. He is truly an example on how to turn a challenging situation into an amazing opportunity to help others. He spares no opportunity to offer advice and resources through his yoga and lifestyle studio—the largest in the Midwest. He is down-to-earth and kind, constantly traveling around the world, learning  healthy living techniques and generously sharing his knowledge in schools and at community events. He is a vegan body builder, which is also quite remarkable. His studio grew from to over 13,000 square feet and from three staff members to thirty—in just four years! What do I admire most about Corey? His broad attitude about life. He allows the wisdom of his own experiences to open his eyes to possibilities.

Steve Fretzin, founder of Sales Results, Inc. honors the fig factors of **discovery** and **passion.** Steve is one of the most enthusiastic people I've ever known. At first glance, he is a successful sales consultant who brings positive results to his clients. Once you have a chance to learn his story, though, you find that his commitment to success actually began in a tragic plane crash that nearly robbed him of his life at the age of twenty-six. Steve was a passenger on board a plane that crashed into a house, leaving Steve immobile for more than two months. During that time, he became aware of life's beauty and discovered a new way of living—one fueled by his passion for sales and making a difference in the lives of others. He went on to lead a successful company, helping thousands of people excel in their jobs. He founded Networking Monkey, one of the largest regional online business networking sites in the Chicago area, and authored Sales-Free Selling: The Death of Sales and the Birth of a New Methodology. What do I admire most about Steve? He took the gift of survival and did something with it.

Lula Esqueda honors the fig factor of **vulnerability.** Lula lost her mother and father on the same night in two different places, her mother to cancer in Mexico and her father to a heart attack in the United States. Five children were left behind in Mexico. Lula was one of the oldest at fourteen. No extended family members fed them, clothed them, or supervised them. They suffered so much from the horrible loss of their parents, often not having food to eat or money to pay the bills. Lula got married and moved to the United States. For years, she and her husband struggled to have a family until finally God gave them a beautiful girl who became their life and reason for living. Lula has an incredible selfless love for her child; you can see it in her eyes. She constantly remembers how much she needed her mother, so she spends as much time as possible with her daughter—who is now about the same age as when Lula lost her mother and father on that fateful night. Lula is grateful for the life she has lived and is aware that her daughter is a precious gift. She rarely talks about her tragedy and is never resentful or angry. What do I admire most about Lula? Lula chose to open herself up and find love after loss. Her sense of vulnerability has helped her find a life built on joy, new possibilities, and her true vocation as a mother.

\* \* \*

The next great story of living the fig factors is yours to write, and it begins the moment you start making an impact on other people's lives. Be aware, alert, and awake to seeing life's true essence and recognizing the extraordinary qualities in the people you love, work with, sit next to in class, pass on the street, or tuck in at night. In this spirit, I leave you with not my words but those of my husband, Juan Pablo. To me, what he wrote best reflects a life reborn again and again from honoring others. His words remind me that each day of our lives has one common theme: when we put the heart of others above our own, we grow. We become inspired to believe in a world without boundaries. We are given second chances on matters great and small, even when everyone else says those chances don't exist.

In a note, tucked in amongst our household mail, he wrote: "To the love of my life, we might be poor, we might be rich, we might live in a shack or a mansion, but we will always be the bridge to this AMAZING love."

# THE 8 FIG FACTORS

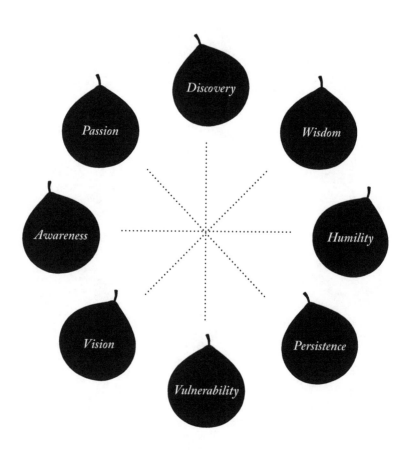

## *About the Author*

Born in Mexico City, Jacqueline Camacho-Ruiz moved to the United States at age 14 where she learned English in just one year. Hungry for knowledge, Jacqueline earned her college degree and became trilingual. From a very early age Jackie devoured amazing literature. Authors like Dale Carnegie, Zig Ziglar, Napoleon Hill and other business icons influenced the launch of her award-winning marketing and public relations agency JJR Marketing in 2006.

A true PR star, Jacqueline's iPhone tells the story: there resides hundreds of phone numbers for top national media personalities, radio/television producers and social media celebrities. She is a regular guest on TV and radio including CBS World News, CBS Chicago, WGN-TV, ABC7 News, WGN Radio 720.

Jacqueline speaks to hundreds of audiences nationwide and is described as having a "fire about marketing and about life that leaps off the stage.".

Jacqueline earned the Emerging Leader award by the Chicago Assoc. of Direct Marketing, the Entrepreneurial Excellence and Influential Women in Business awards by Daily Herald The Business Ledger and was a finalist for Latina Entrepreneur of the Year by the Chicago Latino Network, Highest Human Relations Award by Dale Carnegie, among others. She serves on the board of Junior Achievement- Western Region, Community Contacts and the Publicity Club of Chicago.

As a two-time cancer survivor, Jacqueline possesses wisdom about life well beyond her years. She lives in the Midwest with her husband and business partner, Juan Pablo, and her two children Leonardo and Giulianna.

CPSIA information can be obtained
at www.ICGtesting.com
Printed in the USA
FFHW010653310119
50356001-55455FF